TOO
EMOTIONAL

"*Too Emotional* is both a love letter and a path to freedom for anyone who mistakes their emotions for reality. Reagan's blend of vulnerability and wisdom are a lifeline to those struggling with self-doubt and shame. If you're ready to understand your emotions instead of being overwhelmed by them, improve your relationships, and find the motivation you thought you lost (or never had)—this book is your guiding light."

JESS EKSTROM, Speaker, Author, and Founder of Mic Drop Workshop

"I've found that all creators are different. While every creator encounters roadblocks, some of us have the added challenges of shame and self-doubt. If your emotions have you paralyzed and hold you back from making your contribution to the world, this book is for you."

JAY CLOUSE, Founder of Creator Science

"From an Enneagram perspective, heart types offer beautiful, relational, and emotional gifts. But sometimes, these strengths become obstacles, preventing us from contributing to our communities and our relationships. This book offers a compassionate, positive guide for those who have big ideas but get stuck in execution, struggle to find motivation, or feel ashamed of their lack of progress. *Too Emotional* explores how deep feelers can navigate shame and self-doubt to build the life and legacy they envision for themselves."

STEPHANIE BARRON HALL, Author, Enneagram Practitioner, and Creator of @NineTypesCo

"Unhelpful emotions are the hidden force preventing us from achieving our goals, connecting with others, and loving who we are. For me and everyone I coach, a foundational step for personal growth is the realization that we are not our emotions. Reagan's book is the master class in getting unstuck from unhelpful emotions so we can become unstoppable."

ALEX WEBER, Award-Winning Leader, Author,
and American Ninja Warrior

"I have to admit, I'm someone who doesn't feel enough. This book deepened my empathy for those who experience their emotions more intensely, particularly on my team. So wherever you fall on the 'feelings spectrum,' *Too Emotional* is a helpful guide for anyone seeking to understand and connect with people in their lives who wear their heart on their sleeve."

TIM SCHURRER, Author of *The Secret Society of Success*
and CEO of David Novak Leadership

TOO EMOTIONAL

Overcome the
Thunderstorm of Feelings,
Shame and Self-Doubt

REAGAN PUGH

FOR ELEANOR:

You are my saving Grace

Paperback ISBN: 9798989998708
Hardcover with Dust Jacket ISBN: 9798989998715
eBook ISBN: 9798989998722

SEL042000 SELF-HELP / Emotions
SEL023000 SELF-HELP / Personal Growth / Self-Esteem

Cover design by Karl Hébert
Typesetting by Kaitlin Barwick
Edited by Michael Schroeder and Justin Greer

reaganpugh.com

CONTENTS

PART ONE
When Your Emotions = Reality

CHALLENGES WITH WORK

CHALLENGES WITH RELATIONSHIPS

CHALLENGES WITH SELF-PERCEPTION

PART TWO
The Growth Path for the Too Emotional

FREEDOM FOR YOURSELF

FREEDOM IN RELATIONSHIPS

FREEDOM IN WORK

An Encouragement and a Disclaimer

Build Your Symphony of Support:
Finding the Right Kind of Help

Spring in Austin, Texas, is like walking into a living kaleidoscope of color. The sky is blue and a cool breeze licks at the hairs on your arms. Have you ever found yourself outside on a lovely day, walking alone with your head on a swivel trying to take in all the beauty? You can't stop smiling to yourself because your mood is buoyed by the perfect weather. That's March and April in Austin.

This Sunday afternoon, I'm crowded around a picnic table with my buddies behind one of our favorite bars, having a conversation with some new friends. A group of young men who are part of a leadership program we all have some experience with are passing through town, so we decide to have some drinks before taking them swimming in the springs. We're chatting about life, big decisions, and community.

One of our guests asks me what I'm currently working on, and I share that I'm writing this book and focused on getting it published by late spring. We chat a bit more about the writing process when he notices my buddy Joey standing nearby and invites him to join the conversation. After asking Joey a bit about his work as a therapist, our young guest then wonders aloud if Joey might ever write a book on the theories he's developed as a therapist about people's ability to change.

Joey takes a small sip of his beer and shakes his head while looking over his left shoulder. "Nah, I don't think so," he says matter-of-factly. The young man asks why not, and Joey pats me on the shoulder while saying, "No offense to Reagan's work here, but I just don't think people can change by reading a book."

A few years ago, Joey's comment would have sidelined me for a week. I'd feel so discouraged that I might be inclined to shelve this book project. Maybe you would as well. Perhaps you picked up this book because you, like me, have such a fragile confidence in your worthiness that innocuous comments from friends can cause you to rethink what's important. If so, you're in good company—because we're about to start from the beginning and work through all the awareness, acceptance, and action required to prevent the opinions of others from damaging us so deeply.

But before we do that, I want to make sure to communicate how important it is to find the kind of help you need based on where you are at present.

I disagree with Joey that books can't guide people toward real and lasting change. I can name a couple dozen books— whether they be memoir, novel, poetry, business, spiritual, or self-development—that have altered the course of my life. Some books I reread once a year because they're so crucial to my continued development.

What I think Joey really meant is books *alone* can't completely change a person. And I agree with that.

Throughout my growth journey, I've found it crucial to employ the use of many interventions to support the work of wading through complicated emotions and addressing the corresponding unhelpful behaviors those emotions elicit, including the following:

- Cognitive behavioral therapy
- Emotional freedom technique (EFT) tapping
- Couples therapy
- Meditation training and retreats
- Prayer
- Journaling
- 12-step recovery program (Alcoholics Anonymous)
- Enneagram coaching
- Performance coaching
- Business coaching

There was also a time when my therapist and I were close to starting me on an antidepressant to assist in navigating a particularly difficult season. Many friends who experience the heaviness of life in similar ways as me have shared the importance of psychopharmacological means to support their healing and growth.

Any one of the interventions mentioned above couldn't have supported me in isolation. Journaling alone could never have supported my need for spiritual connection through prayer. Meditating by itself could not have totally guided me through the anxiousness I've felt about my business; a business coach was needed. And, yes, only reading books about depression and addiction would not have been sufficient if not paired with talk therapy and working a recovery program.

It's imperative that we learn to recognize what we need and determine which resources will enable us to take care of ourselves in a healthy way. I ask you to be conscious of this as we begin our journey together. This book is written for people who experience overwhelming emotions, bouts of depression, anxious thoughts, and negative perceptions of themselves and their life situation. It's heavy stuff, and I hope to join your symphony of support by drawing on my own experiences, professional advice, and expert insights in this book.

But I would implore you to first seek help from a professional if you're hurting. Then we'll journey together toward awareness, freedom, peace, and more positive participation in your life and relationships.

PART ONE

When Your Emotions = Reality

Hijacked by Emotions

When you're in a bad mood, there's nothing worse than being surrounded by a few dozen loud, happy, dancing people. As we start our journey together, that's exactly where you find me: in my own personal hell, crammed inside a crowded dance hall in Luckenbach, Texas.

The mustachioed fiddle player on stage is finishing a solo, and the whole band's getting ready to come back around for the chorus. I'm sitting alone on the edge of the room while nearly every other soul two-steps and twirls across the knotty planks in this smoky, beer-sour building in the middle of nowhere.

The band wraps up their set and hops off stage for a quick break as my boss shuffles over to our table, sweaty and smiling. "There's a group of moms over there who are out for a girls' night, and there's no *way* I'm gonna manage to dance with all of them," he says with a grin.

I look at him for a long moment. He's having the time of his life twirling every member of this middle-aged, bedazzled mom squad. But I just don't see the point.

Because, remember, I'm in a bad mood.

He downs his stale beer as he scans the room, then turns back with a grin: "Oh man, they spotted me. Hey, get us another pitcher. I gotta get back out there."

He holds his glass out for me to grab. I take it and exhale as loudly as I can. Taking no notice of my exasperation, he starts back across the dance floor, then stops and pivots back to the table.

"Or . . . you could join us? They're a blast, man. One of them can teach you how to two-step. Come on, we drove all the way out here." He tries with no luck to invite me into what was supposed to be a fun diversion from our work.

After waiting a beat, he silently accepts I'm checked out for the night. He knows what I'm doing. He's been around me when I get hijacked by a bad mood and has learned to just let me stew instead of cajoling me into joining the dance.

He boogies away, the music starts back up, and I hug the wall as I head toward the bar for a fresh pitcher. Walking back to our table, I get elbowed, bumped, and hip-checked half a dozen times, sloshing beer all over my wrist. I curse all these people with dumb smiles on their faces who seem to have figured out the part of life that continues to elude me: how to participate and enjoy moments regardless of how I'm feeling inside.

I also curse my boss for dragging me out here and for having a good time—especially considering we had a frustrating day of work.

We're on a planning retreat and rented a little ranch house in the Texas hill country for a few days of focus, but we just can't seem to find any clarity on this current project. We felt like we were banging our heads against the wall all day, so my boss proposed we blow off some steam and go out for cold beer and dancing.

I agreed to the cold beer part, not the dancing part.

At this point in my life, I hate dancing. I'm no good at it, and to me, dancing doesn't make any sense. It's just a distraction invented by people who want to avoid having meaningful conversations. Also, I'm worried I'll make a fool of myself, and on a deeper, unconscious level, I'm concerned that I'll open myself up to criticism. What if I don't do it right? On rare occasions, emboldened by alcohol, I'll get on the dance floor. But tonight, I don't want to drink that much because we have another day of planning tomorrow.

Looking around the dance hall, I can't understand how some people are able to compartmentalize their lives, let go of their feelings, and put their energy toward something else—like having a good evening—even when life is full, and work is stressful. I'm jealous of my boss for enjoying himself even though he has a hundred more things on his plate than I do.

Come to think of it, I'm jealous of all these folks merrily spinning beneath this rusty tin roof. Every one of them has a whole life to balance and worry about, yet no one but me seems weighed down, pissy, or hijacked by their emotions. They've all chosen to be present and do the things you're supposed to do when you're in Luckenbach, Texas, on a Thursday after dark.

As the night carries on, I finish the entire pitcher of beer by myself, and my boss is nowhere to be seen. I sigh. *We'll probably be here for another hour at least*, I think. Now I'm unhappy with him all over again for dragging me out here. I'm also unhappy with all these people for not behaving how I wish they'd behave—I wish they'd just settle down a little bit.

Underneath it all, what I don't yet realize is that I'm unhappy with *myself*.

If you stumbled across the blog I kept during this season of my twenties, all you'd read about is how I value intentionality and living an adventurous life. This was my aspirational identity. In conversations, I'd quote passages of poetry about seizing the day and making every moment count. I'd claim I want my life to be a story worth telling. Yet here I am again, trapped by my emotions and stuck in a mood. I'm not seizing the day. I'm actively choosing to *not* participate in my life. I'm unhappy with myself because I *know* I'm being a stick in the mud. I'm a pro at getting in a funk and letting everyone know it.

My boss experienced the same stressful day, and yet somehow he manages to be playful while I'm melancholy. Missing out on my life because of my unpredictable emotions is, sadly, an almost daily occurrence.

LEARNING TO OBSERVE OUR FEELINGS WITHOUT BEING OVERCOME BY THEM

Don't worry—I didn't drag you into this dance hall with me without a purpose. But before we go any further, I want to make sure to tell you this book isn't about me changing who I am—and I certainly don't want you to change who you are. Our growth path involves learning to accept who we are, not trying to be someone different. Then, from a place of awareness and acceptance, we can get to work.

Back at that dance hall years ago, I'm cycling through unhelpful feelings while my boss is having a grand time precisely because I lack that awareness and acceptance. I don't yet *consciously* know I'm unhappy with myself. I'm just experiencing a slew of messy feelings, and focusing on them seems more important than enjoying the evening.

Why can't I break free from my emotions and participate in this moment? Why can't I just dance? I wonder if you can relate.

Have you ever felt like you don't belong in the room with people who seem at ease with themselves, others, and their life at present? Do your desires for a rich and meaningful life ever seem misaligned with the way you actually choose to live it? If I stood up from my lonely table and walked outside that dance hall to get away from all the happiness, would I also find you in the parking lot doing the same—solitary, sulking, and looking to the stars for answers?

If you're nodding to yourself—if you might be the other moody person standing on the sidelines of the fun zone—this book is for you.

Picture this with me for a moment: There we are, standing with our sizable emotions among those unlit Texas hills, refusing to participate in the dance because for some reason we don't *feel* like participating. Though we may notice one another, we don't acknowledge it. People like us prefer not to acknowledge that anyone could ever feel the way we feel (more on this later). So, we settle on brooding alone together while the music plays and the dancing continues in the building behind us.

Now imagine, after a long while, we decide to speak to one another. Maybe we bum a cigarette off the old cowboy fiddler and chat about why we've both decided to spend our evening as outcasts instead of having a go at making a positive memory. How might we explain what's keeping us off the dance floor?

At first, we'd likely offer surface-level observations because we don't trust each other yet.

"I'm just one of those people who takes life a little more seriously than others," I might say. "I have a hard time getting hyped about going out dancing."

You might exhale and nod your head. "Sometimes I'm just in a funk and I need people to stay out of my way until I'm ready to reengage."

I'd chuckle in agreement.

For a while, we'd probably commiserate about all the things other people do that frustrate us. Then, perhaps, we'd go a bit deeper and be a little more honest.

Maybe, as I look out past all the sleeping cars in the gravel parking lot, I'd admit to you that when something happens in my life that causes me to react emotionally, I put all my energy toward wallowing in that feeling. I think I need to understand everything I feel, and I punish anyone who attempts to pull me back into the present reality.

You'd nod for me to continue. Accepting your invitation, I'd say, "Here's the crazy part: I secretly want others to pay attention to my sulking and invite me to join in—but I make them work for it. Not even totally sure why I do that."

That's where you chime in, "Yeah, sometimes I can't see through what I'm feeling. Forget inner peace, healthy relationships, and excitement about work or whatever. I just want to understand why I'm always a moment away from melancholy."

Of course I relate to that. We're both essentially trying to express the same thing, even if we can't find the perfect words. We believe it's more important to pay attention to our subjective and unpredictable emotions than to accept and participate in real life right in front of us. As a matter of fact, we have come to believe our emotions *are* reality.

People like us are dominated by our feelings.

Conversely, those not like us will, more often than not, do anything they can to escape an emotional flare-up. They'll find a distraction, get back to work, laugh it off, surround themselves with people, go on a run—whatever they need to do to hit the reset button.

But you and me, we dive deeper into our feelings and the mood they elicit. Damn anyone who tries to interrupt our pity party! I use my emotions like a suit of armor (at least I rationalize that stewing in them is self-protective). I don't yet know what they're protecting me from on this sticky Texas evening, but I'm clearly interested in keeping my distance from anyone and everyone urging me to boot scoot and change my behavior.

Are you still with me?

Does it ever seem like you can't find freedom from your funky feelings, and you're envious of everyone else who seems to be "normal," unencumbered, and content? You don't want to live a blissfully ignorant life, but you wish you could at least do more with your energy besides wallowing in your pain.

If you and I are similar, here's the sad truth about our default way of operating:

- We like our emotions.
- We like our problems.
- We like our negative narratives.
- We like the sense of separateness we feel from others.

Even if we complain about how bad we feel, the truth is we like it all.

Well, maybe we don't *like* it all, but we're clearly committed to our default way of operating. We must be getting something from believing our emotions represent reality because we keep practicing the same behaviors. But while we're busy juggling our emotions, what's really happening is we're missing out.

If you're with me so far, you know very well that being trapped at a dance hall after a bad day with zero desire to dance isn't the only place our emotions hijack reality.

We get hijacked by our emotions everywhere and every day.

This affects our schoolwork, job satisfaction, and career trajectory. Our preoccupation with our feelings can keep others from fully participating in their best possible life as well (which we'll talk about later). It keeps us down on ourselves and unable to see our gifts and love who we are. The good news? The presence of big emotions isn't a dead end. We just need to understand why we devote so much energy to our feelings and learn how to observe them without judgment. Awareness and acceptance are the way out.

CHAPTER 2

What We Miss by Putting Our Feelings First

*Confronting the Source of
Our Emotional Turmoil*

It's nearly 4:00 a.m. and I'm jarred from sleep by my wife, Elle, who is inadvertently jabbing me in the ribs as she crawls to the head of our bed to peer out the window. I pretend to remain asleep a moment longer, hoping she'll settle down. Minutes later, Elle is still surveying the darkness outside our bedroom. I grunt and finally ask her what's going on.

"The motion-activated lights in the backyard turned on," she whispers with the morning breath of a velociraptor. "And before that, I think I saw a flashlight shining through the windows."

Welp—that does it. I don't know about you, but people snooping around my house at night ranks high on the list of things that will rouse me from slumber. In a flash, I'm up and cupping my hands around my eyes, trying to identify whatever danger is encircling us.

Seeing nothing immediately outside our bedroom windows, I grab a flashlight and walk out the back door to assess the backyard and garage. Nothing. *These intruders are very sneaky.*

I charge back inside and into the front room, where I shine my flashlight through the window to check the side gate, which connects our front yard to our backyard. It seems to be shut and fastened.

Then I see it. Our compost bin has been knocked over. *Must be a raccoon*, I reason to myself. I recall a moment a few weeks prior when, taking the trash out after dark, I happened upon a fat ringtail sitting atop the compost bin. It hissed at me before scrambling up the nearby fence and plopping into the backyard.

It's definitely a raccoon.

I march back to our bedroom, announcing to Elle there's no need to worry, it's merely a raccoon, but she's already asleep again. To even the score, I poke her ribs to wake her up so I can inform her it's probably a raccoon. "That's what I thought," she yawns as she rolls over.

I exhale, close my eyes, and try to breathe deeply. But my heart is still pounding in my chest. *I mean, I think it's a raccoon, but what if it's someone on the run from the law and they're using our backyard as a hideout?*

On the run from the law? What is this, a western? I rebuke my anxious imagination and turn onto my side, nearly chuckling, when I hear a scrape against the window.

I'm on my feet again, rummaging through the sock drawer for a pocketknife. I also grab my phone to record the whole ordeal just in case these are my final moments and I'm not around to tell my story. I curse myself for not yet drafting a will.

I go all the way outside this time and find nothing. There I am, barefoot in my underwear with a pocketknife, looking no more intimidating than a confused, unclothed wood whittler with insomnia.

I head back to bed, but rest does not come to me. A little while later, a police siren wails nearby and I'm sure the cops are about to drop from helicopters into our yard and apprehend the murderer hiding in the bushes. A half-hour later, our old house settles and creaks a few times, convincing me there's someone upstairs. *They've been in our home the whole time?* I whimper to myself.

My instincts are on high alert. Every sound, every shadow, every anxious thought and feeling of dread demands my attention and receives all of my adrenaline-fueled energy.

Thankfully, dawn finally arrives and we're not dead. I let our Labrador Retriever, Lily (who, by the way, was good for *nothing* during the most terrifying hours of my life), out for her morning bathroom break. I saunter over to pick up the compost bin and wonder why I spent so much energy attending to unsubstantiated fears all night long.

For those of us who often find ourselves overcome with negative emotions or unpleasant moods, our daily experience is not unlike reacting to imagined intruders in the night. Think about a time you've been disappointed by someone, or got your feelings hurt, or found yourself feeling shame for not being motivated or disciplined enough.

Or trapped in a crowded dance hall deep in an inescapable funk. When we're experiencing unpleasant feelings, we're reacting to an external event we believe requires our attention. Whether it's a passing comment from a friend or colleague or a missed deadline at work, we feel an emotion to deal with a situation we don't like—which is natural, by the way. Some people have learned to witness their emotions and determine whether they're helpful; people like you and me, however, we can sometimes be fooled into believing the messages from our emotions are real. And, just like my fearful state on the night of the raccoon, we later find we got worked up over nothing.

Although we might "know" our emotions shouldn't always consume our attention, we just can't help but pay them mind. Our instincts are screaming and our bodies are telling us these emotions must be sorted out before we can go on living any sort of peaceful life. As a matter of fact, we've come to believe that, if we are to survive, our emotions must be experienced. We've been trained to feel everything our instincts tell us to feel.

That's what we're supposed to do, right?

Wrong—that's what we've been conditioned to do.

This is where things can get confusing, because sometimes our emotions have enabled us to thrive. It is true that our emotions have benefitted us by allowing for deep connection with others, making life feel richer, or enabling us to produce creative work. Yes, we know from experience that being attuned to our feelings can sometimes prove helpful. No doubt there are plenty of occasions you've tapped into your emotions to be creative, empathetic, or intentional. These are all good things.

But we're not beginning this journey together to celebrate how our emotions are occasionally helpful. You and I are on this page right now because sometimes our feelings get so big they interrupt our ability to focus, practice objectivity, take action, maintain healthy relationships, make meaningful contributions at work, and participate in our lives.

We're here because we're tired of hoping for a life that feels smoother and less dramatic yet finding ourselves down in the dumps because we can't seem to shake free of our moodiness. We want to stop getting stuck in our feelings and grow.

The first and most difficult step of all personal growth is shining a light on the parts of ourselves that we'd prefer to keep hidden. This self-awareness doesn't come easy, but it's the key to our freedom.

To move forward, we've got to uncover the reasons why we behave the way we do. This means we've got to confront the puppeteer of our outsized emotions: our ego.

For the purpose of this book, when discussing the ego, I mean our sense of self. Our ego reflects the personality we've constructed to survive in the world. For people like you and me, our ego is behind the priority we place on our ever-changing emotions. The ego is not interested in our freedom from emotions but our addiction to them. This is because our ego, like every other living thing on planet Earth, is interested in one thing: surviving and thriving.

And for our ego to thrive, we can't. It's that simple. We must remain the same. Our ego prefers the status quo, and its discomfort with change deeply influences our perspectives, opinions, defense mechanisms, habits, mindsets, and attitudes. To put it simply, your ego doesn't want you to spend your energy on growth; it wants you to spend your energy rejecting growth.

As a writer, speaker, and coach, I've had the privilege of working with thousands of students, entrepreneurs, employees, CEOs, and regular ole folks who want to grow—and every single one of them is interrupted by their ego. For some, their ego keeps them trapped in anger. Others are confronted with anxiety or a desire for control. Everyone deals with a villain in the form of their ego that robs them of peace—and ours hatches emotional traps that cause us to feel shame.

Hear this: It's not your fault that you experience outsized emotions that can overwhelm you. Something happened to you at some point which caused your ego to create a story that the only way you can survive life's challenges is by dipping into a funk, overly identifying with a mood, distancing yourself from others, getting your feelings hurt, wallowing in shame, and judging everyone from a distance.

"Our ego is designed to keep us safe and comfortable, but it can hold us back from new experiences and personal growth," Dr. Tara Swart, a neuroscientist, former psychiatric doctor, and senior lecturer at the MIT Sloan School of Management, notes in her book, *The Source: Open Your Mind, Change Your Life.* "We need to become aware of how our ego operates and learn to balance its need for safety with our desire for growth and change."[1]

This isn't to say it's impossible for us to expand our minds. In fact, that's precisely what needs to happen for us to make those critical breakthroughs that change our lives.

In his well-known work on the interior world of humans, *The Structure and Dynamics of the Psyche,* psychiatrist and psychoanalyst Carl Jung similarly emphasized the importance of recognizing and transcending the limitations of the ego. "The greatest and most important problems of life are fundamentally insoluble. They can never be solved but only outgrown," he wrote. "This 'outgrowing' proves on further investigation to require a new level of consciousness. Some higher or wider interest appears on the horizon and through this broadening of outlook, the insoluble problem loses its urgency."[2]

I say again, there's nothing wrong with our having an instinctual desire to cling to our feelings; that's self-preservation at work. But if we don't choose to evolve we will stagnate, or worse, go backward. When our emotional ego is working so hard to protect us from progressing in our lives, I'm sure you can agree we may be surviving, but we are certainly not thriving.

When our ego is satisfied by our predictable behavior—like when we get our feelings hurt or feel shame—we subconsciously experience a sense of control and certainty. *Ah yes, this feels right, this is familiar!* But what we often forget is that our default response to stressors in life might provide security, but it doesn't allow for joy, connection, or peace. We trade freedom for familiarity.

As miserable as it seems, this loop is curiously hard to escape. It's easier to keep feeding the ego than to realize we can break the stronghold of our emotions by reacting differently than we've been programmed to. Behaving in new ways requires us to question the truthfulness of a lifetime of deeply held feelings and beliefs. It's more straightforward to wake up each day and keep living the same old story where we're the misunderstood victim of a life we can't seem to navigate in a more carefree or positive way.

When our emotions come first, we can easily lose sight of what matters most and struggle to make important changes. Maybe you've found it hard to summon the motivation to exercise, shake a bad mood, or believe in your abilities because you don't *feel* like you can do any of those things.

Consider difficulties you experience in your interactions with others. In your relationships, do you take offense when it's not intended? Maybe you worry about the perceptions people have of you, or doubt anyone ever has, or ever will, love the *real* you, which causes you to feel like you're not worthy.

Or view your lived experience from the standpoint of a job or school. Maybe you feel unable to muster the energy to meet a deadline or study for a test. Perhaps you just can't seem to find the courage to make a creative contribution, or don't embody a sense of purpose because you don't *feel* particularly energetic, courageous, or purpose filled.

For those of us whose daily experiences are directly connected to our current (and ever-changing) emotional state, life can be shaky, discouraging, unpredictable, and depressing.

Well, I have something important to tell you: Your feelings are real to you, but they don't represent reality.

Read that again.

Profound and meaningful change starts with the decision that you're ready to practice awareness and confront your ego so you can find freedom and peace. Only then can we begin to see with clarity how much we've relied on our emotions to validate the behaviors preventing us from participating in the present moment.

If admitting and addressing that seems like a lot of work, it is—but so is the alternative.

THE EXHAUSTING STATUS QUO

Learning to be more objective about our feelings and to think critically about our unpredictable moods may sound daunting. For perspective, however, we need only consider the grueling work required to continue on with our lives, unchanged. How much more difficult will our lives be if we continue sinking into an emotional tailspin anytime we're challenged?

Meaningful change starts with becoming aware of how our outsized feelings are working overtime trying to protect us from imagined threats to our already fragile sense of self-worth. When we understand this, we can make a critical, concerted choice when our ego attempts to convince us that our default emotional reactions represent reality. Will we fall victim to our feelings again or focus on the facts?

Put another way, we can decide whether we engage our emotions or experience reality as it is before us. Instead of making the same survival-based decisions, we can choose to grow beyond our ego with the newfound understanding that we don't need to respond to its incessant attempts for our attention. More importantly, we can learn to have compassion for ourselves for believing we need to react in such extreme ways when we feel uncomfortable.

OK, deep breath. Enough pointing out all of our short-comings for a moment. (Although, they're not really short-comings, just reactions we're going to learn to release.)

Hear me on this too: There's nothing wrong with you because you feel big emotions that get you down. You're not the only one whose ego has convinced them their emotions constitute reality. Who knows what very real wounds you've experienced? I'm not here to invalidate moments you've been hurt, which may be the underlying cause of your melancholy disposition and lack of faith in your ability to participate in your life. The overwhelming feelings you experience when stressed could be your ego's way of trying to protect you from more harm. So be observant, not hard on yourself. People like us don't need to carry any more shame.

The goal here is not to criticize your past behavior but to bring awareness to your current way of operating and urge you to ask one simple question:

Is my tendency to believe my emotions represent reality (which prevents me from participating in the present moment) helpful to me, my relationships, and my work?

Notice something about this question. We're asking if our current behaviors are *helpful* or *unhelpful.* That's important. We're not worried about what's good or bad here; we don't need to experience our own growth as a moral endeavor. You might already be way ahead of me. "Duh, of course I spend time wallowing in unhelpful emotions instead of enjoying my life," you may say. "But that's just what I do because I'm a damaged wreck of a person."

Hang with me. We're going to work on that sense of defectiveness. But we have to start simple by learning to see our tendency to exit reality in real time. Awareness is the way through, and acceptance is the vehicle.

Here are a few ways I've learned to bring awareness to my emotions, which may be of service to you. Notice when you are feeling or doing any of the following:

- Checked out of the present because you feel a certain way
- Obsessing over areas in your life you believe are lacking
- Ruminating over ways others have hurt or offended you
- Questioning your value, potential, or worth
- Unmotivated to engage in work, life events, or relationships
- Wondering what others might be thinking about you
- Comparing yourself to others

- Fantasizing about a future when things will be better than now
- Reliving a past when things were better than they are now
- Dreaming of a creative project, but never seeing it through
- Experiencing impostor syndrome or self-doubt
- Feeling defective, misunderstood, or broken
- Hopeless about your future
- Disappointed in yourself and your contributions

Can you recall times you've missed out on life because you've been busy experiencing one or many of the bullets above? What private, simple moment of joy, like reading a book at a coffee shop, was hijacked by emotional overwhelm? Can you think of a holiday where you missed out on the fun because you felt misunderstood by a loved one's side comment? Have you failed to make progress on your creative idea because you're still obsessed with your feelings of self-doubt? What joy might you be forgoing because you're so preoccupied with feeling every emotion you experience instead of getting busy living?

If you suffer from unchecked emotional swings like me, you might scoff at the idea anyone else could ever understand your particular brand of sadness, melancholy, or self-doubt. But I hope I've articulated your life experience accurately enough to earn a sliver of your trust so you'll hear me when I say you're not alone. I understand. And there is a version of your life where you can learn to do this instead:

- Witness your emotions instead of feeling them.
- Assess whether they are a realistic response to your circumstances.
- Refocus your attention and move forward.

People like us can sometimes find it difficult to engage in this work because we mistakenly believe we must *feel* motivated to do it—and when we're in a fragile emotional state, we feel *anything but* motivated. So we're going to move slowly here at the beginning. The simple practice for this chapter is noticing your tendency to withdraw and reading this aloud to yourself:

I'm currently allowing my emotional state to cause me to misinterpret reality, and I'm choosing to prioritize experiencing feelings over participating in my life.

Remember, our egos are insatiable. Our subconscious mind is fearful of losing our identity when we change. So, as we move forward, your instincts will try to convince you that every single emotion rooted in fear and doubt is worth engaging.

Let's commit right now to stop directing our energy toward remaining the same, and instead forge a path toward freedom through practicing awareness and acceptance.

REVISITING THE DANCE HALL WITH A NEW LEVEL OF CONSCIOUSNESS

Looking back at my dance hall pity party with more clarity, I can now see the unconscious decision to be in a mood wasn't serving the function I thought it was. In reality, those protective emotions showed up to get me out of dancing because I was afraid of doing it wrong. I feigned seriousness so my boss might learn to take me seriously, and I pouted because one of my tried-and-true coping mechanisms used to be getting attention by presenting as unhappy—all kinds of energy-sucking behavior. Further, I can now see how wallowing in those feelings of inadequacy kept me from living my life, making new memories, and learning how to be the kind of person who can savor any moment.

If I'm being really honest, my emotional response to my boss's invitation to enjoy an evening of drinking and dancing gave me an excuse not to challenge my ego's default programming. I could avoid doing the work of participating in my life and sabotage the potential opportunity of finding new evidence that I am worthy, interesting, and capable of being playful. I used my armor of emotions to skip out on new experiences like I always did when I was uncomfortable.

Consider this: While your emotions might feel difficult, continuing to engage them is actually the easier way to navigate your life. That's because super emotional people like you and me are professionals at experiencing our emotions as reality. The harder work involves zooming out and seeing the whole picture and choosing to behave differently than we did last time our thunderous feelings gathered overhead.

Please know that I'm not patronizing you by saying I'm proud of you for making it this far. Trust me, I hate it when people think they understand my particular experience without knowing my whole story. I honor your feelings, emotions, and struggles and in no way want to minimize them or cause you to feel like you're weak or behind in your own development.

We emotional types are all searching for something, and when we can see that our emotions aren't really going to give us what we need, that's the first step. The next step is about realizing how our overly emotional reality causes us problems in the workplace. People like us are plagued by a lack motivation and self-sabotage, and we fear others' opinions of our contributions. But we can change.

Let's keep moving.

NOTES

1. Tara Swart, *Open Your Mind, Change Your Life* (London: Ebury Publishing, 2019).
2. Carl Jung, *The Structure and Dynamics of the Psyche* (Princeton, NJ: Princeton University Press, 1972).

CHAPTER 3

In Search of Motivation

Big Dreams, Little Work

I groan like a man much older than my twenty-two years as I fiddle with printer cables beneath my boss's desk. *This is the definition of wasting my God-given talents,* I think to myself as I reconnect my boss's laptop to the printer—again. This makes three times this week she's needed my assistance to print something. *Why can't people over the age of fifty understand technology?* Finally the printer starts whirring, and I return with an air of importance to my desk, where I plan to do nothing until it's time to leave for the day.

It's 2008, and we're at the height of a recession. I'm a recent college graduate with a creative writing degree who avoided doing any sort of career exploration before graduation. So I've returned to my hometown to join a family friend's nurse staffing agency. Despite my dissatisfaction with the role and the shame I feel because I've moved back in with my parents, it's not a bad gig. They're paying me more than I'm worth. My boss even lets me create my own title, so I choose something lofty: director of business development.

But the only thing I've developed in the nine months I've held this job is an unreasonably strong resentment for anyone who expects anything of me.

I should be grateful for the opportunity to work at all; I basically do whatever I want. Each week, I present a marketing plan and a few ideas for developing business, and they're happy to pay me. My hang-up is the work doesn't *feel* like it *means* anything. What do I care about making sure hospitals have enough nurses? My life story is supposed to be more substantial than this.

So instead of applying myself at work, I learn how to game the system. I get to work early to fool everyone into thinking I'm invested even though I'm not. I take a full hour for my lunch break and spend the hours of 3:00 p.m. to 5:30 p.m. on Facebook or reading blogs. When I'm out on sales calls, my lunch hour often stretches to ninety minutes because I read self-help books in my parked car or call friends who are still in college living the dream.

On some days I feel guilty for my half-heartedness, but quickly rationalize the guilt away. *If my work was only more fulfilling*, I tell myself, *then I'd be invested.*

Everything would click if I could only find a job more suited to my skill set or a project that ignited my passions. If I had the freedom to explore more creative endeavors, then I'd figure out how to harness the discipline I seem to be missing right now.

But this is not true.

You see, I had the chance to explore my passions and work on an inspiring project just about a year before, and I squandered that opportunity. Let's go back there for a moment: We're in a big athletic arena at my university. The lights are bright, the crowd is quiet, and I believe every word I'm about to say.

"So that's why I'm moving to Hollywood to become a screenwriter. I know it won't be easy—but our lives aren't meant to be easy. As I begin my new adventure, I encourage you all to live boldly and tell good stories with your own lives."

I walk back to my chair on the stage to the sound of applause and take my seat next to the provost, who elbows me and whispers, "Amazing news! I can't wait to watch one of your movies!"

It feels good.

I'm twenty-one years old, I'm student body president of my university, and I'm wrapping up a well-received term. I frequently give speeches—like this one to graduating students who are about to receive their class rings—and I feel important.

I'm on top of the world.

Walking back to my dorm to change before heading out to meet friends, I scarcely consider that I've not spent more than a few hours working on a script. I've not spent a single day of my college career on or around a movie set. I've never written one screenplay. Yet, I rationalize, I'm good on stage, right? I acted in a summer theater troupe between sophomore and junior year, so why not set a lofty goal for the purposes of swindling affirmation from people I don't even know?

After graduation, I decide to delay my trip to California and remain in my college town—drinking every night and working for a local businessman who thinks I have promise. He's started his own newspaper, and I'm writing articles for him about the history of San Marcos, Texas. Between working for him, nursing hangovers, and enjoying the last vestiges of college life, I don't write a single word of a screenplay. I don't make any progress toward my dream. The quiet work of cultivating inspiration, putting words on the page, learning about screenwriting, and connecting with people in the industry seems like an unfair trade for a career I thought I wanted. Every time I sit down to write something, I'm plagued with doubt and uncertainty because the path seems so unclear and daunting—plus my ego is incessantly asking the question, *What if you're not any good?*

As summer comes to a close, I still haven't booked a flight to Hollywood. I have no script to shop around. With wounded pride, I move into my parents' garage and take the job where you found me at the beginning of this chapter—working for a family friend in my hometown. Instead of an exciting adventure on the West Coast, I'm driving five minutes to work, then back to my childhood home to sit in front of the TV, hide my drinking from my family, and wish I was in college again.

What's more, I repeat this pattern multiple times over the next fifteen years:

1. I claim I'm going to do something cool.
2. Fantasize about how amazing it will be.

3. Collect affirmation from others by telling them about the idea.
4. Suck all the joy I can out of the fantasy.
5. Avoid the hard, quiet work of starting and finishing the job.
6. Feel shame for not being someone who finishes things.
7. Pick something else to fantasize about.

It's taken my whole life—at least to this point—to get clear on my issue with work, discipline, and productivity. I tend to avoid the hard, (seemingly) meaningless work required to find fulfillment, make a significant contribution, or satisfy obligations I don't feel inspired to complete. I'd rather people validate me for my ability to create an inspiring vision or for being the unique and special person I am without having to earn it. *If only people could see how much potential I have on the inside, then things would work out differently,* I lament to myself.

Does this sound familiar?

- Do you get excited about ideas, yet crumble when it comes to execution?
- Do you become bored with menial tasks and tell yourself you're suited for greater things?
- Do you envy others who finish projects and complete their work?
- Do you jump from fantasy to fantasy without ever doing anything in real life?

- Do you make decisions about your life and work based on what will garner praise?
- Do you wallow in shame and experience deep self-loathing due to inaction?
- Do you think others must have it easier than you, because how else are they able to thrive?

People like you and me who experience life through our emotions first can face an uphill battle in professional or academic settings—both of which are biased toward action (doing) and intellectual horsepower (thinking), not feelings.

Thankfully for us, emotional intelligence has become more celebrated in the workplace. On-the-job experience and research demonstrate how being in tune emotionally can boost productivity, increase the quality of contributions and deepen work relationships. But we've still got work to do; emotional intelligence goes beyond celebrating feelings. It requires us to understand our emotional reactions so we can more deftly approach our interactions with others and better understand our external world.

Emotional intelligence is really "an ability to recognize the meanings of emotions and their relationships, and to reason and problem-solve on the basis of them," as researchers John D. Mayer and Peter Salovey explain in their book, *Emotional Development and Emotional Intelligence: Educational Implications.*[1]

For us, I want to emphasize the work is not to simply experience feelings but to apply what we learn and to take action. Our emotions can be a superpower if we learn to recognize them, process them, and move forward. But we can't expect any of this to just happen—we must work at it, and the challenges are real. Namely, our misguided belief that we must direct our energy toward feeling our feelings *before* we can apply our mind to tackle a challenge or summon our will into action.

It's not that we necessarily desire to avoid using our brains or taking action so we can dance with our feelings, but when one is wired the way we are, melancholy frequently overtakes motivation. This is confusing and frustrating because we have a big, heartfelt vision for who we want to be and the life we desire. But feelings of insecurity, hopelessness, and lack of motivation often overshadow our ability to realize our aspirations.

There's nothing wrong with wanting to enjoy our work, looking forward to the day our skills allow us to accomplish great things with ease, and appreciating external affirmation. Yet sometimes there seems to be a deep chasm between what we want down the road and what we're willing to do right now. We fantasize about an ideal future and avoid the work we must do to get there. This leads us to sometimes deem difficult, tedious tasks—like reconnecting your boss's printer *again* or writing pages of a screenplay—to be meaningless. We lose steam and settle for feeling familiar emotions of self-doubt and victimhood instead of taking small steps toward growth.

If you find yourself nodding along, whether you experience this lack of motivation consciously or unconsciously, something is inhibiting you from making big progress toward the life and work you desire. Your ego wants to lock you up in feelings of inadequacy instead of committing to the work at hand. To overcome this, we must become more aware of our emotions, embrace them when necessary, and—this is the hard part—learn when they are not accurate depictions of reality, so we can chin up and get to work.

The first step in this direction is learning to notice how our preoccupation with our feelings about work prevents us from summoning motivation.

FIXATED ON FEELINGS, ALLERGIC TO ACTION

Imagine there's a hidden camera trained on you as you sit down to work. You could be at the office, your desk at home, in a hotel, on an airplane, at a coffee shop, or in a coworking space or client conference room. Wherever you are, pretend we can see you as you prepare to tackle the tasks you want to accomplish. What would we observe?

I don't know about you, but if a hidden camera were to capture my workdays for most of my career, you'd see an amalgamation of the following scenes:

- Sitting down to work in an emotional haze, followed by lots of nesting to make the place just right. That could include getting a glass of water, unpacking my bag, putting a napkin underneath my iced Americano, finding the right song to play, and lighting a candle.

- Looking around to take in the emotional state of the room if others are around, whether they be coworkers or strangers; there's a period of observation and comparison.
- Checking my phone to make sure there aren't any text messages I need to address and skipping over the ones I'm avoiding.
- Doing the same with emails. I respond to the ones that elicit the kind of emotions I'm interested in experiencing right now and avoid those I don't feel like answering.
- I might visit my favorite news websites, pull my phone back out to check social media, then look at my calendar to prepare myself emotionally for what's going to happen today.
- Perhaps then I'll start to create my to-do list if I haven't already. This process begins to overwhelm me as I think of the things I need to do and wonder whether or not I'll feel like doing any of them. Sometimes I'll put the to-do list down and journal for a while to make sure I capture all of my feelings.
- Then I'll return to the to-do list. However, if I'm still feeling anxious and emotionally unprepared to begin the day, I'll try to create a sense of calm. I'll do this by engaging in inconsequential tasks I believe will allow me to feel more motivated, like doing chores and life stuff. If I can get the house right, or finally book those

concert tickets, or clip my toenails, or give the dog a bath real quick, then I'll be able to focus on my work. Of course! I can't focus right now because I need to do some life maintenance.

- After folding the laundry or refilling a prescription or calling my mom back, I still don't feel motivated. But now a bit of time has passed since work was supposed to begin and I'm starting to feel guilt and shame, so I need a distraction to help me feel something different. Time to read the news again, check my bank account, review text messages, and watch the trailer for the next Marvel movie that just dropped.

- Ugh. After a half-hour of this, I still don't feel any better, and I'm certainly not any more motivated than I was when the day began.

- Well, it's probably a good idea to take a walk, listen to a motivational podcast, or meditate. Anything to avoid a shame spiral. Maybe I should change clothes and go on a run, shower, then restart the day. Or I could take a power nap or grocery shop to help reset my feelings so I can finally begin my work.

- About this time fear sets in because the day's halfway gone, and I have meetings in the afternoon. It's time to start worrying about the people I'm meeting with and what they think about me. Cue the internal movie projector replaying all the times I've disappointed people and embarrassed myself by not living up to my potential.

- This fear of what others think motivates me to halfheartedly finish a presentation just in time for the meeting or call where I'm likely defensive because I believe everyone is trying to uncover my lackluster effort or mediocre abilities.

- After meetings conclude, it's time to finish the day even if there are a few hours left. We're throwing in the towel. To make myself feel better I'll envision how I'm going to wake up early tomorrow before anyone can bother me, light a candle, write in my journal, and get myself in a good emotional state before beginning the most productive day ever— *tomorrow.*

- The very next morning, the circumstances are perfect. The candle is lit, the music is right, and I've turned off the internet connection to my laptop. No one can bother me. It's just me and the work at hand.

- I begin with a bit of excitement about where things might go, but slowly you might notice my eyes glazing over, my shoulders dropping, and my head tilting as I gaze absently into the corner of the room. *What if this thing I'm working on ends up being no good at all?* I'll think to myself.

- Instead of utilizing the morning and taking advantage of the blank canvas I thought I needed, I'll feel a sense of inferiority before I do much of anything at all. I spend the rest of the day chasing my emotions and making very little progress.
- Sadly, more or less, the next day is a repeat of the days and weeks before.

Do you wince as you read any of the bullet points above? If so, you're in good company.

Take a look back over the list. What is the common theme across all my failed attempts to get to work? In one way or another, the scenes above feature a person who is dominated by their feelings and believes no work can happen until a perfect state of emotional equilibrium is achieved. Going deeper, the scenes above show us someone who would rather decode their fickle emotions than take action because they're terrified of what might happen if they were to step out of their internal world, ignore their ego, and participate. Will things go well? Will they go poorly? It doesn't matter. The risk of trying something new and the uncertainty around what emotions we may encounter are enough to keep us stuck in the no-action zone.

Again, we don't necessarily want to avoid work. We're not trying to be lazy or take advantage of our employers or clients. We have big dreams for our lives and a deep desire for a meaningful vocation. We're simply fixated on our feelings, which causes us to be allergic to action.

We fantasize about a perfect workday where we feel all the right emotions which will allow us to make our best contribution. But like my summer after college graduation, which was supposed to be spent writing a screenplay, we often squander the perfect circumstances.

But why?

By now I hope you can admit external circumstances are not to blame for your lack of professional progress or wavering commitment to a creative endeavor. Circumstances have nothing to do with our missing motivation—it's our feelings that block us from taking action.

Our feelings continue to show up and interrupt our actions because there is something else at work. Deep down, our ego is doing its best to prevent us from leaving our internal world in order to participate and contribute. It whispers to us: *Stay small, stay quiet. Even though avoiding your work or procrastinating on a meaningful personal project causes you feel shame, at least you'll never risk being rejected for trying to contribute and not receiving affirmation for your efforts.*

We dream of fulfilling vocational opportunities, yet curiously miss daily chances to move toward our goals. As we explore what's behind this, we'll realize that a lack of motivation is not the true culprit.

NOTE

1.   John D. Mayer and Peter Salovey, *Emotional Development and Emotional Intelligence: Educational Implications* (Basic Books, 1997).

CHAPTER 4

A Call to Action

Why Participation Beats Motivation

Andrew, an old college buddy, gives it to me straight. He lets me know in no uncertain terms that I'm missing something essential.

"You just have to find your killer instinct, man—where is your killer instinct?" he asks rhetorically, pushing his finger into my sternum.

We're in our late-twenties, and Andrew is in town for work. We've met up for drinks, and he's trying to encourage me to be braver and more engaged in my new job with a consulting firm.

Andrew is the most loyal of friends. Few others believe in me so fiercely. He's one of those guys who picks up the phone no matter what he's doing, answering with: "Is everything OK? You need anything?"

People like Andrew look after the rest of us and put us all to shame with their work ethic. You know the kind of person I'm talking about, don't you? They're Type-A, action-oriented doers. They're a hammer, and everything else is a nail. They have boundless energy and are always motivated to get their work done. They're builders. And I'm jealous of every one of them.

The personality typing tool, the Enneagram, teaches us that we utilize three different intelligence centers: our head, heart, and gut. Some people (like you and me) operate from our heart and emotions, some run off of logic and brainpower, and others are fueled by their gut and have an instinct for action.

Take a wild guess which one Andrew is. He's a gut type driven by action. When I sent Andrew a draft of this book for people whose complicated feelings prevent them from participating in their lives, he texted me within ten minutes (and this is a direct quote):

"Trying to understand the goal of the book. Is it to just help highly emotional people get through life?"

He couldn't understand it. People like Andrew have a different relationship with feelings and emotions. They're not as easily distracted by how they feel. Instead, they use feelings to fuel them into action. On days when I just can't seem to focus or find motivation to do my work, I look at people who can use their gut to drive them to take action, or their head to solve the challenges in front of them, and I lament with this heart full of feelings, *It sure would be nice if I were wired differently.* This is one of our first obstacles when it comes to finding motivation. We waste time wishing we were different instead of choosing to change our actions.

Back to the bar where Andrew still has his finger lodged like a dull bayonet in my chest.

As he does his best to "encourage" me, I begin to experience all the shame and doubt I feel every time someone tells me I just need to dig deeper for motivation or try harder even if I don't feel like it. I look past him, back into the corner of the bar. A guy and girl are playing darts—looks like a first date. They loose darts into the air, and even their worst shots manage to lodge into the cork. All around everyone seems to be enjoying themselves, and I imagine they all must have it easier than I do. *They must all be more normal than me,* I think. *Why can I not seem to get excited about tackling the challenges of a new job?* I almost whisper, as I duck my nose into my nearly empty glass of beer.

Andrew orders another round and kindly recounts successes I've had, encourages me, and tells me what he's learned from me. After building me up, he shares some examples of routines that enable him to be productive. I appreciate this, I do, but I resent him at the same time for reminding me how easy it is for him (and seemingly everyone else) to take action while I lay in bed trying to talk myself into getting up and engaging with the day.

Some days we can find motivation, but it doesn't seem to last, does it? Other folks I work with who regularly experience big emotions and a sense of inadequacy echo these sentiments.

One individual I've coached says:

"I know what I'm supposed to do each day, but I believe I need to feel motivated to engage, so I do a bunch of things I believe will put me in the right space. I meditate, I journal, I clean up the house, I watch an inspiring video . . . and the next thing I know it's lunch and I haven't done anything, so I just write the whole day off and feel an immense amount of shame."

For us "action-repressed" folks, it's not that we're unable to take action; we just operate from our hearts, which means our motivations are different from others. We want to feel emotionally connected to what we do. We don't care about getting things done as much as we desire to feel whole and complete before beginning our work. We've got such negative stories we tell ourselves about our potential or how others will receive our work that we can't seem to push off the starting line without being in the perfect emotional state.

The problem, as you likely already know, is that waiting for the perfect emotional state will mean days, weeks, and even months of missed opportunities toward progress. Then the stories you tell yourself will only get worse. So how can we overcome a self-defeating pattern of procrastination? At the risk of showing all my cards too soon and you abandoning this book early, I'll go ahead and tell you the big growth theme for you and me: participation.

Participation trumps motivation every time. Motivation is the ship that will never come in—at least not in the way we want or when we most need it. So for us to find fulfillment in our work, we're going to have to start taking action first. This, in turn, will change our thoughts and cause us to finally feel like we have the ability to get things done and make a significant contribution.

OUR DEFAULT WAY OF OPERATING
Feeling → *Thinking* → *Doing*

THE PARTICIPATION PROCESS
Doing → *Thinking* → *Feeling*

This radical reworking of how we approach daily tasks and challenges may feel counterintuitive, especially since many of us don't believe we're capable of seeing tasks through to completion. But changing our approach is the only way we'll change. I find inspiration in the timeless wisdom from Norman Vincent Peale's *The Power of Positive Thinking*. "Action is a great restorer and builder of confidence. Inaction is not only the result, but the cause, of fear," Peale tells us. "Perhaps the action you take will be successful; perhaps different action or adjustments will have to follow. But any action is better than no action at all."[1]

While working for the nurse staffing agency, I never experienced the joy of growth because I didn't take action to uncover where my strengths might have existed. I just gave up and wrote off the entire job because I didn't feel motivated to do work I deemed meaningless. Who knows what kind of screenplay I could have written if I actually put words on the page. Instead, I depended on my feelings to drive the creative endeavor and came away empty-handed.

In your job or career, I wonder what frustrations you continue to experience because you're mired in your feelings instead of focused on your particular responsibilities. By participating in small and simple actions, we can alter the way we think, which changes how we feel—but we must get started.

You still might have your doubts, just as I did, about your ability to engage with work that seems uninteresting or misaligned with your unique giftings. Behavioral research suggests, however, that it's not only possible but also self-reinforcing. Regardless of our particular disposition, we know humans in professional settings are enriched by one element above all others: progress.

Researchers Teresa M. Amabile and Steven J. Kramer describe this "progress principle" in their 2011 *Harvard Business Review* article, "The Power of Small Wins." They had workers involved in a range of projects that all involved creativity—from inventing kitchen gadgets to solving complicated IT problems—catalog in daily diary entries their feelings, their motivation levels, the work they did, and what stood out in their minds.

"Of all the things that can boost emotions, motivation, and perceptions during a workday, the single most important is making progress in meaningful work," Amabile and Kramer note. "And the more frequently people experience that sense of progress, the more likely they are to be creatively productive in the long run. Whether they are trying to solve a major scientific mystery or simply produce a high-quality product or service, everyday progress—even a small win—can make all the difference in how they feel and perform."[2]

Instead of chasing a feeling, take action. Let what you build step by step and piece by piece push you forward.

"Motivation often comes after starting, not before. Action produces momentum. If you can start, you'll often find that motivation will follow," writes author and speaker James Clear in his bestseller, *Atomic Habits.* "This is why a bias toward action is so important. When you don't feel like doing anything, the most important thing is to do something small. Build momentum and then trust that motivation will come later."[3]

For those of us searching for the mysterious source of motivation, and who yearn for progress to quiet the old voices of inadequacy and shame, we have a clear imperative moving forward: participate through taking action.

Of course, as important as it is to understand this deeply ingrained relationship between actions, thoughts, and feelings, we all know it's not as simple as flipping a switch. We're not just action-repressed are we? We also worry about what others think of us. Perhaps the biggest reason we fail to take action is that we don't want to waste energy doing something wrong, then receive negative feedback. In other words, we still need to address our interior motivation for procrastination.

Let's go there next.

NOTES

1.   Norman Vincent Peale, *The Power of Positive Thinking* (Prentice Hall, 1952).
2.   Teresa M. Amabile and Steven J. Kramer, "The Power of Small Wins," *Harvard Business Review* (May 2011), https://hbr.org/2011/05/the-power-of-small-wins.
3.   James Clear, *Atomic Habits* (Avery, 2018).

CHAPTER 5

But What Will People Think?

Our Struggle with Feedback

I've just launched my solo speaking business, and I'm trying to build some momentum. In an effort to market myself and publicly share more about the topics I speak about, I build a few personal development workshops that I plan to run on Zoom.

One workshop I'm particularly excited about is titled "How to Stop Thinking About What Others Are Thinking About You." After spending years worrying about others' negative judgements, I've finally mustered the courage to buckle down and build a workshop I'm excited to offer. Rarely am I proud of my work, but this session feels honest and brave. I believe it will benefit people like me.

When it's ready to go, I advertise tickets for the workshop by posting about it on my Facebook page:

"How often do you find yourself worrying that everyone in your life is constantly sizing you up? You've got great potential and you desire to contribute, but you feel paralyzed because you're worried about everyone's secret criticism of you . . . you just feel stuck before you even begin."

A few people purchase tickets. Several friends like or share the post, and I begin to feel encouraged about my future as a speaker. But then, tragedy strikes. Some random person comments:

"I've literally never experienced that. Why would I waste my time thinking about what other people think?"

I read the post several times as sweat rolls down my back. Each time I mouth their nasty words, I doubt myself even more. I'm mad at myself for ever believing I could make a career of public speaking, and at this commenter for not seeing the value of my workshop. I think, *How could this person publicly shame me for trying to support those who fear criticism?*

In the span of a few minutes, I've already convinced myself that I shouldn't build or deliver workshops anymore. Time to pick a new career. I've decided I'm moving to a small town in Iowa and taking a job as a barista at one of those Starbucks with a limited drink menu located inside a grocery store. I want to disappear. I envision everyone I know seeing my Facebook post and the public rebuke I received from a stranger. I imagine all of them on a private text thread joking about my sensitivities and desperate attempts to launch my own business. To put it mildly, I see my whole life blow up in front of me.

Imagining the demise of one's entire career is heavy stuff. Sadly, during this season of my life I'm making a habit of it. Just two days earlier, I contemplated my own worthlessness in a similar fashion—that's when I received some less-than-stellar feedback about a proposal I sent to a potential client. Yeah, this whole "try something, get feedback from others, choose to get wounded, and believe the world is coming to an end" thing is my *jam*.

If you're anything like me, the shame-fueled self-loathing that leads to self-sabotage is a regular occurrence in your work life too. You know what it's like to build up the nerve to really invest in a project or new role only to be deflated when you discover others don't believe *everything* about your contribution is perfect. And let's be honest, even when you get gold stars across the board, you don't enjoy that either. You secretly wonder if everyone is being genuine or praising you out of pity.

Those of us who have big feelings also have big fears. If we detect even a slight hesitance from others to validate our contributions, we'll trash an entire endeavor before it sees the light of day. Whether prepping a presentation, mopping the floors, organizing an event, building a financial model, or writing a book, we often bail when there's a risk that feedback from others might reinforce our fears about our lack of potential.

Sound familiar? This was my spiral when I went from being Hollywood-bound to homebound, moving back in with my parents after college. Here's how the pattern tends to play out:

- You get inspired and have a heightened emotional experience. The world seems to make sense. You have a new vision for how to contribute—whether it be a side project or your job. You imagine how your old demons would be healed and your future self would be whole if you could pull this idea off.

- You dream up a bunch of strategies in a feverish creative storm. You begin to hope that maybe this time you'll actually be able to hold on to inspiration long enough to produce something you actually share with your coworkers or community.

- Perhaps you string together a few days of disciplined work. You even manage to do the mundane things you hate, and you're so excited about your progress that you want to start talking about what you've got cooking. After all, you need some external affirmation if you're going to sustain this momentum.

- Upon sharing your big idea with a few people, you find yourself frustrated with them for not experiencing the same excitement you felt when inspiration first struck. You might even share with them that you're frustrated. You quickly change topics and reject their offers to help refine your concept. Screw them for not "getting it" right off the bat.

- You then return to your idea with a bad taste in your mouth and modify it until your unique touches are no longer visible. You settle for producing something without heart and resent the world for it. Or you abandon the idea altogether and produce absolutely nothing at all. Now you're more convinced than ever that you're not the kind of person who can create, contribute, or collaborate.

How many solid concepts have you abandoned because people didn't pat you on the back for merely talking about an idea or taking the first few steps toward action? How often have you divested your energy from a project at work because your teammates don't overwhelmingly agree with your perspective or approach from the start?

Why are criticism and feedback so hurtful for us? It almost doesn't make sense. After all, we're already rather glum and melancholy folks who beat ourselves up sufficiently each day. We've built a tolerance for bleakness. So it's strange that a bit of constructive feedback or the risk of an idea not panning out could send us into hiding. This all begins to make more sense when we dig deeper into our underlying fear.

Remember, participation is one of the core aspirational virtues of this book, so exploring what drives us away from participating is a central focus for our work together. As we discussed previously, action is the antidote to our lack of motivation. This is easy enough to accept when we simply don't *feel* energized about our work. But our challenges are often deeper than that. What if we're hesitant to take action because we fear others will either think we're doing it wrong—or worse, that we have nothing of value to offer?

It's worth considering that the reason we lack motivation, tend to avoid action, and shy away from putting big effort into professional contributions is because we are afraid we don't have what it takes to participate at the level of others, and that we never will. Our ego is doing its best to protect us from this fear. So instead of progressing by trying and learning from feedback, we often eject from the game altogether. Or we hedge on personal projects and make mediocre or safe contributions in the workplace. We'd prefer to receive tepid feedback on efforts to which we never fully committed over the risk of putting our hearts into the work, only to be told we've come up short.

As complicated and unique as your relationship to work might feel, this is classic growth mindset versus fixed mindset stuff. Growth mindset research, popularized by psychologist Dr. Carol Dweck in her book *Mindset: The New Psychology of Success*, explores how our abilities can be expanded if we're willing to learn and put in the work.[1] When someone practices a growth mindset, they come across as motivated, action-oriented, and resilient in the face of feedback.

They believe more experiences lead to more growth. They're not concerned with what others think because they're more interested in learning.

The opposite—which more often than not describes people like us—would be someone operating from a fixed mindset. Folks with a fixed mindset avoid effort and lose motivation easily because they don't believe they can develop. Any feedback they receive is not seen as information to improve but more evidence that they are irreparably flawed.

To put it simply, when practicing a fixed mindset, one believes they have no ability to grow or improve. They feel stuck at their current level of ability with no hope for a future where they might thrive in the face of challenges and get excited about the work required to grow. When practicing a growth mindset, one trusts their potential to develop is as deep as their willingness to keep showing up and participating with a spirit of curiosity.

Of course, simply knowing we'd be better off practicing a growth mindset doesn't do much, does it? It's hard to focus on picking the right mindset when we're plagued by worries that our greatest fear—that our contributions aren't sufficient because we aren't sufficient—might be validated anytime we try. This fear is so real that there actually is a psychological term for it: fear of negative evaluation, or FNE.

In their article, "Perceived fit and feedback avoidance: Examining the role of fear of negative evaluation," published in the *Journal of Educational Psychology*, Melissa W. Rudolph and Seung Hee Kim find: "Individuals high in FNE may avoid negative feedback to protect their self-image, which can result in reduced learning and performance. This avoidance is particularly likely when the feedback is incongruent with their self-concept or when it threatens their sense of identity."[2]

People like you and me are often overtaken by our emotions and mistake how we feel for the objective reality of our circumstances. This is because our ego is fighting to keep us safe by spinning up an emotional tornado to protect us from the perceived dangers of taking feedback a little less seriously and participating in our lives. As a result, we often have a difficult relationship with work (where we have to do things in real life) and can struggle with motivation. We know we need to take action but have a difficult time doing so because we worry our efforts will be met with a lackluster reception, or worse, feedback that might affirm our fear that we don't have anything valuable to offer—and that causes us to feel shame.

Deep breath.

Am I onto something?

If you're feeling overwhelmed—don't. There's nothing wrong with you. It's only natural for folks like us to feel bad when our ego tries to protect us. So let's not feel shame about our shame. Let's instead cultivate some awareness and acceptance so we can move forward.

We must learn to see through the hopeful fantasy of easy work and recognize our instinctual urge to hide behind fear and self-sabotage will get us nowhere. What if we accepted that our contributions don't have to be perfect, well-received, or 100 percent unique for them to matter? Ultimately, our greatest healing will come from participating, contributing, and finishing what we begin, regardless of what others think.

Believe it or not, for folks like us who choose to engage in the work outlined in this book, the actual *doing* becomes the easy part. (Can you believe it?) It's managing our shame and subsequent self-sabotage that requires the most attention. No one is out to get us when they react, or don't react, to who we are or what we contribute. We must remember the voices echoing against the walls about our lack of talent, skill, vision, creativity—those voices are our own.

In thinking about the application of this idea, I can't help but wonder what might happen if each of us believed we're a little bit better than we think we are. What if we all trusted that, based on our own life experience, we always have something valuable to offer, even if others have different opinions about our contributions?

In an interview on Krista Tippett's podcast *On Being*, researcher and author Brené Brown says belonging (read: confidence) must first happen inside of us before we can receive it from the world. Brown says, in her experience, the strongest people "didn't negotiate it [belonging] with the world; they carried it internally; they brought belonging wherever they went."[3]

This book is born out of a nasty battle with shame and self-sabotage. In order to complete it, I enlisted the help of some twenty readers who provided feedback on each chapter. I did this before I was ready and in spite of my fear these ideas might be rejected. The responses I received from readers weren't all praise. Many individuals shared critical feedback and differed in their opinions on what should and shouldn't be included. But I learned to see the perspectives of others aren't dangerous and can sometimes provide valuable direction. These pages, written for people like you and me, are a living example of how we can put things into the world and request feedback without spiraling into shame and sabotaging our efforts.

My perspective won't resonate with everyone or even a majority of people (like my buddy Andrew), and I've come to accept that. But my hope is that if you feel overwhelmed by shame or other unruly emotions, you can draw strength from my experience of putting my best contribution into the world. I hope you can see areas in your life where you bow out before you even begin because you think you can't participate until you are 100 percent ready and are guaranteed to receive only positive responses.

If this book is truly for you, I hope it has helped you feel seen so far. You're not defective for being the way you are, and you can manage your response to self-doubt. There is a way for you to participate in work without emotions wreaking havoc and preventing you from taking action and learning along the way.

NOTES

1. Carol Dweck, *Mindset: The New Psychology of Success* (Ballantine Books, 2007).
2. Melissa W. Rudolph and Seung Hee Kim, "Perceived fit and feedback avoidance: Examining the role of fear of negative evaluation," *Journal of Educational Psychology.*
3. Brené Brown in "Strong Back, Soft Front, Wild Heart," *On Being with Krista Tippett*, February 8, 2018, https://onbeing.org/programs /brene-brown-strong-back-soft-front-wild-heart.

CHAPTER 6

Reworking Our Relationship with Work

I'm sitting in the safety of my car, parked across the street from a gym that's housed in an old converted warehouse. Through the rusty loading bay door, I'm watching a woman throw chains over her shoulders and proceed to do pull-ups. It looks like she's completed fifteen, which is more pull-ups than I've completed in fifteen years. I'm shaking my head, mouth agape, and I'm terrified.

Oh my goodness—I'll never be able to do that, I think.

The sun is just beginning to poke over the horizon as birds whistle and traffic picks up. "I could bail right now and no one would ever know," I whisper.

Breakups make us act strangely, don't they? In my relationship that just ended, I felt insecure and unmasculine. Now that my ex and I are finished, it's time to prove to myself (and her?) that I'm a manly man who can keep up with high-performing athletes. I hold my breath and get out of the car. I timidly walk across the street and through the parking lot toward the house of pain.

This is one of those gyms where former Marines work out. People are doing weighted triceps dips with 45-pound plates strapped to their waists. They're scrawling their names on sign-up sheets stapled to the wall advertising weekend retreats where one can shoot assault rifles and skin animals. As I enter the building, I think I see Dwayne Johnson finishing up a set in the corner—but it's not him. It's just Vin Diesel.

My goal is simply to get to the point where I can keep up with a regular training session at 100 percent intensity. I'm starting from zero, so I begin training privately with one of the coaches to learn the movements and get clear on my baseline. After a half-dozen sessions and lots of overpriced protein powder—which my trainer scoops into a baggy from his personal, unmarked tub sitting in the trunk of his car—I'm ready to hit a regular class.

It rocks me. No joke: I finish a 6 a.m. class and somehow make it home, get back into bed, and sleep until noon. I wake up to see my boss has called eight times, fearing me dead. In the following weeks, I participate in a few more sessions. Although I'm not having to take naps anymore, I'm still stumbling to my car, laying the seat back, and trying not to black out for a few minutes before turning the ignition.

I find myself frustrated at how much of a toll this work is taking on my body. I think, *I'm so out of place.* I'm flooded by all of the fears I developed as the kid who hit puberty very late and never felt particularly athletic. I begin to wade back into thoughts about my own defectiveness and my inability to become a better version of myself.

You know how this goes by now, right? Let's recap what we've covered:

- I am overcome by emotions and believe they are reality.
- My ego tries to protect me by keeping me in those emotions instead of participating in new experiences.
- This causes me to lack the motivation to do anything but wallow in my feelings.
- In reality, I'm fixating on my feelings instead of taking action.
- And I'm overly concerned others will judge my feeble attempt to participate before I'm a pro.

We emotional, sensitive, melancholy folk must come to realize that deliverance from our shame isn't glamorous. We are freed by engaging in the mundane, uncomfortable, boring, repetitive work of participating. We have to remember that everyone's a beginner until they're not, and trust we'll find meaning along the way. This goes for educational pursuits, careers, workouts, cooking, relationships, gardening, training pets—you name it.

Early one morning after a series of brutal sprints, I'm lying on the floor in misery next to a giant industrial fan. A veteran gym-goer I've seen before sits down nearby with a groan, rests his elbows on his knees, and asks how I'm doing.

"How the hell do you think?" I cough. "I've been coming here for almost two months so I can stop being terrified by exercise, but each session reminds me of how much I can't hang."

He smiles and says between his own labored breaths, "Just so you know, man, this doesn't get any easier—physically, anyway."

He lies down next to me, and we cool off in silence, our sweat darkening the mats underneath us.

In the car on the drive home, I think to myself, *What a crock of shit. Here I am doing this because I believe one day I'll unlock the next level of athletic ability and be able to perform feats of strength with ease. Where are my results?*

Up to this point, I've believed there is a fitness nirvana one reaches. In this elite state, you stop getting lightheaded, you never have tunnel vision, and it ceases to feel like you're pushing scalding magma through your veins. I've believed that if I can force myself through the miserable action of showing up to the gym then maybe, just maybe, I can stop being such a crybaby in my regular life and learn to take action in my career.

Nope. That isn't how it goes, according to my sweaty gym friend. Instead, you just learn to commit to a process of doing something unattractive and unpleasant in the short term, regardless of how embarrassing it is, and trust you can handle the difficulty. Then eventually you learn to believe something totally different about yourself and your abilities.

BEHAVIORS SHAPE BELIEFS

Over time, new behaviors create new beliefs, and new beliefs change the way we feel about ourselves. You see that? Behaviors (actions) can directly influence our beliefs (thoughts), which can create a new emotional experience (feelings). If we want to feel differently about our potential, our work or our abilities, we must prioritize new behaviors.

Even behavioral changes seemingly as minor as smiling through discomfort can affect our thoughts and feelings. That's essentially what researchers Tara Kraft and Sarah Pressman found in their aptly named study, "Grin and Bear It: The Influence of Manipulated Facial Expression on the Stress Response," published in *Psychological Science.*[1]

In the study, researchers discovered that even when participants didn't feel happy, choosing to smile changed their emotional state and decreased their levels of stress.

Participants put a small device in their mouth that caused them to involuntarily smile or frown. With the device in their mouths, participants were then asked to complete a challenging task. Before and after the experiment, their stress levels and emotional states were measured.

The findings reveal that those who had a smile forced onto their face experienced more positive emotions and lower levels of stress than the frowny bunch. More so, the smilers showed increased activity in the parts of the brain associated with positive emotions. Small behavioral changes affect not only emotions but what we believe to be true about ourselves.

I've learned over the years to enjoy waking up early by telling myself I enjoy waking up early, then actually getting out of bed when the alarm goes off. I thank myself each morning when I finish writing my daily 750 words, acknowledging how important that behavior is to me. I'm improving my meditation practice by sitting for longer periods of time and choosing to view myself as someone who values meditation—because I *do* the thing.

I enjoy work when I'm willing to focus on the small building blocks of making a quality contribution. Executing on the little things tells my brain I can do work, which makes me feel like showing up again. Contrast this with my old mode of operating where I'd fantasize about the apex of my career and feel discouraged by the chasm between where I'm at and where I want to be.

Our actions tell us who we are.

When we decide to act as the person we wish to be, our brain begins to believe that maybe, just maybe, we're capable of doing the next hard thing. There's an important distinction to make here: we begin to realize we're *capable*, we're not magically *comfortable*. Because action doesn't get easier. Not for me, not for anyone—even those ripped gym rats I envy.

Something changes in me when I finally accept those crazy gym workouts aren't a walk in the park for anyone. This awareness pulls me out of my emotions and helps me realize maybe there's nothing particularly wrong with me because I struggle with motivation. Perhaps waking up each day and taking action is hard for everyone in some way. I'm not the only one who feels challenged by new things or nervous about looking foolish. Maybe exercise is supposed to be difficult. After all, we need to tax our muscles to get stronger, right?

I'm learning we don't get the gifts of health, purpose, courage, or a fulfilling career until we take small actions that resemble those desires. We can't have the life we want without putting in any of the work.

When we're willing to unseat our emotions from mission control, we can take a more objective approach to the same activities that once sidelined us. We develop new ways of thinking about trials and challenges. Participating in difficult pursuits or pushing through the mundane middle of a work project strengthens muscles inside our brains and allows us to believe we too can make progress.

But we can't do this if we're chasing the hope that one day all the hard work will be over and whatever challenging thing we want to master will become effortless. We can't do this when we're convinced we have to feel confident to march onward. We'll never accept our capabilities if we hide in our cars because we're afraid of some imagined judgment we might receive while trying to get better at something.

For us romantic types, we can (and should) still put our hearts into our work, just not the way our ego instructs. Think about it this way: Let's stop trying to force ourselves to do things (like exercise) we falsely believe we'll never like out of guilt or shame. Guilt and shame might spur us into action in the short term, but we won't create sustainable practices when fueled by such negative sources of motivation. Instead, we can make it our objective to fall in love with the practice of whatever it is we endeavor to do. We can learn to see the obligations on our plate as ends in and of themselves and remember that more feelings won't deliver us from unpleasant feelings. Action does.

When we stop believing we'll be delivered from the pit of pain if only we can get into the right emotional state, we can avoid the greater pain of unmet expectations for ourselves. The rabbi and philosopher Abraham Joshua Heschel emphasizes this important distinction between loving practices and loving results in his essential book on rest, *The Sabbath*. As he elucidates, "There is happiness in the love of labor, there is misery in the love of gain."[2]

The beautiful, paradoxical magic of all this is that when we focus on valuing the ingredients of the outcomes we desire, the outcomes we thought we'd never achieve become even more meaningful—because we enjoyed the journey. When we write because we've come to value the process of writing, we produce clearer, more imaginative words. When we exercise because we've learned to enjoy testing ourselves with small struggles, health becomes enjoyable and part of our identity. When we have a bias toward action because we know taking action helps us rewire our brains, we learn our feelings aren't reality and we start living independently of our emotions.

The only way to learn to love something or someone is to put in the hours through action. I'm sure you can think of instances in your life where even the prickliest of people endeared themselves to you after you persisted in the relationship and looked for more generous ways to interpret their tendencies. I'm betting you are proficient at something today because you put energy into the process rather than simply longing for an aspirational outcome, like finding joy weaving piano scales together instead of just dreaming about Carnegie Hall. But this takes time. The work doesn't get any easier. We simply learn to rise to the big challenge of valuing tiny tasks. Instead of fixating on our fantasies about how great our career, business, or sense of job satisfaction will be one day, we fall in love with the small activities we get to perfect along the way. Even if it means reconnecting your boss's computer to the printer—again.

These days, I don't go to the gym with Vin Diesel anymore, but I am steadfast in my regimen of uncomfortable and boring practices. That includes writing, running, and picking up the phone. I'm also learning to cherish the daily opportunity to fall in love with thankless work.

Our growth from this point is completely dependent on our willingness to march forward into the unsexy assignment of being a regular person with a regular job living a regular life without any concern for the way others happen to be living. I can imagine someone like you or me abandoning this book right here, right now. We don't want to live a regular life learning to take regular actions—we want to live a meaningful life! We don't want to be normal, we want to be special! We don't want to become another cog, we want to chart our own path!

Well, dear reader—and I say this with all the kindness in my heart—if your life, relationships, or work were going to plan, you probably wouldn't have picked up this book in the first place. Like my action-forward pal Andrew, you would have questioned the very need for it. But you're still here because there's a disconnect between what you want and what you've been willing to do up to this point.

I come to you in peace as someone who wallowed in emotional turmoil for over a decade wishing I could be the perfect combination of gifted, special, unique, and creative. I dreamed of being the person who takes two months of vacation per year, who is also famous and commercially successful but, of course, hasn't sold out. I've scoffed at the standards of "regular" people, while also desiring to be accepted for totally regular contributions. I've desired rich relationships without putting in any effort, and I've believed my life is supposed to be full of meaning just because I think it should.

But one day—and I hope for you, that is today—we wake up and realize our hopeful desires have been unreachable because of our belief that we must feel something before we can do something. It is the choice (conscious or not) to prioritize our emotions that keeps us from taking action and leads us to hide from feedback. When we instead tackle the mundane tasks before us and focus our energy there rather than on how we feel or what others think, we rework our relationship with work. We chart a new course.

You are charting a new course. Onward!

NOTES

1. Tara L. Kraft and Sarah D. Pressman (2012): "Grin and Bear
    It: The Influence of Manipulated Facial Expression on the
    Stress Response," *Psychological Science* 23(11): 1372–8; doi:
    10.1177/0956797612445312.
2. Abraham Joshua Heschel, *The Sabbath* (NY: Farrar, Strauss and
    Giroux, 1951).

CHAPTER 7

All About Me

Lost in an Internal World

Kevin and I walk into the residence hall a few buildings over from ours, pass through the lobby doing our best to look like we live there, and locate the room rumored to be the party spot.

He looks back at me with the excitement of a paleontologist standing in fresh dinosaur tracks as he opens the door. We cautiously enter. The air is thick with angst and freedom. Our shoes squelch across the sticky floor, and we can barely see by the faint pulsing of colored Christmas lights stuffed into asbestos ceiling tiles. The sparse furniture has been shoved out to the edges of the room, and twenty or so youths shout at one another over Mike Jones on the speakers.

It's my freshman year of college. Kevin and I were randomly paired together as roommates, and this is my first time venturing into the uncharted waters of university life.

Hours earlier, Kevin pleaded with me to join him for a night out. I finally relented and resolved to do my best to make friends.

Shortly after walking into the party, Kevin abandons me to talk to some girls, so I make awkward conversation with a group of strangers. Fast forward one hour, and I'm still listening to six guys talk about Ultimate Frisbee, college football, and spearing wild hogs. *Dear God, spare me.* During a lull in the conversation, in an effort to connect more deeply with everyone and speak about something of substance, I ask a few of the guys within earshot what they think these years in college are adding up to.

The guy next to me squints and starts pouring whiskey into my empty cup. "What's it all adding up to?" he asks.

"Yeah . . ." I mutter, wishing I could take my words back. I know exactly what's about to happen, but continue anyway. "Like, when you think about this stage of your life, what is the big theme? What are you learning? What are these moments now telling you about who you are becoming?"

One guy appears to shift his eyes comically from side to side as he chortles into his drink. Even the posters of Johnny Cash and Kurt Cobain, which hang askew from the dorm room's cinderblock wall, seem to be in on the joke. The guy pouring liquor into my red Solo cup tops me off with a shout, "There! That should get you into party mode because, dude, I don't understand *anything* you're saying!"

Everyone laughs as they quickly find a reason to turn away from our failed conversation. Kevin returns as the circle is dissipating, quickly realizes what's happened, and drops his head with a groan.

"Oh no. You tried to pull them into the deep end, didn't you?"

Like a concerned parent, Kevin goes on to remind me that college parties are not the place for self-actualization. He patiently explains *again* that he's learned to stomach my obsession with the meaning of life, but: "We're at a party, numbnuts—give us a break."

I force a smile as I normally do when others don't seem to understand me, feeling a bit wounded and discouraged. Then I drift away inside myself and forget about that room and those people.

These days at university are the days of going on long, lonely walks, sitting under live oaks, and journaling at the coffee shop hours before other students wake up. Early on in my college career, I develop the belief that I'm no good at traditional red Solo cup parties because I'm the guy asking big questions about why we're all here. I want to explore the depths of our inner experience with others, but everyone else seems content doing the opposite.

This causes me to feel like an outsider. I sense I'll forever be misunderstood, which becomes a theme in my life. It feels like my need to be seen, heard, and acknowledged for my perspectives and interests is at odds with the modus operandi of the absentminded masses. As hard as I try to connect with others, there seems to be a chasm between us.

"You're not in one of your funks now, are you?" Kevin says, snapping me back into the moment.

I look at him through the fog of my own feelings. "I don't know. I think I'm gonna go for a walk." I set my drink down.

"OK man, but you gotta figure out how to do parties!" He slaps my butt as I walk through a crowd of careless peers and make my way out of the building, across the quad, past the quiet lecture halls, and deeper into myself.

My girlfriend is at a concert with a friend visiting from out of town, so I have nowhere to go. Back in my dorm room, I stay up late writing in my journal and reading Thoreau's *Walden*. I whisper his words with reverence to myself by lamplight:

"I wanted to live deep and suck out all the marrow of life, to live so sturdily and Spartan-like as to put to rout all that was not life, to cut a broad swath and shave close, to drive life into a corner, and reduce it to its lowest terms, and, if it proved to be mean, why then to get the whole and genuine meanness of it."[1]

I nod off to sleep, and Kevin stumbles in hours later, waking me up to whisper through a shower of beer spittle, "You missed one helluva party."

The next morning, I'm up and out before first light with my camera to catch shots of fog rising from the springs near campus. I breathe deeply as the sunrise buries itself into its own reflection under the quiet waters. This solitary life feels right to me, and for some reason, my way of living seems to puzzle everyone else. My dad tries to encourage me during an early-morning phone call by saying I probably just haven't found my people yet—to keep looking and putting myself out there.

This seems impossible.

So, despite my deep desire for meaningful connection with others, I resolve to stop trying to make friends and decide to swim in the deep end by myself for the rest of freshman year. The recesses of my internal world feel more welcoming than the external world; at least when I turn inward, there's a greater likelihood I'll avoid rejection and get my needs met on the depth, meaning, and substance fronts. In the life experience I've gathered thus far, the external world and the people who live in it rarely guide me to the marrow of life Thoreau instructs me to pursue.

It's become clear my needs and interests are at odds with others'. Believing I'm separate and different becomes my ego's way of protecting me from the pain of rejection and the sadness of being misunderstood.

The thing people don't tell you when you're the young sensitive person asking big life questions is that eventually many people will take interest in their own internal worlds, which will create opportunities to connect in meaningful ways. But for a while, it sure feels like you're lost. It seems like everyone else got the map on how to traverse one's formative years with ease—except you. So now you're off course and wandering through the mist of some dark forest. But, after the initial shock of separation, you realize you're quite content alone. You settle into the sounds of your own solitude as you continue to wander. The lostness and loneliness soon become welcome friends, because they enable your friendless exploration of the safer world inside yourself.

So far, we've brought awareness to our tendency to believe our emotions are our reality. We've taken an honest look at our fixation on feelings and are beginning to see how we can get trapped in shame when we receive what we perceive to be negative feedback from the world. This causes us to hide and draw inward instead of taking action by participating in our lives or making contributions in our work. Not only do the tendencies we've covered affect our work, they most certainly take a toll on our interactions with others.

A research professor at the University of Houston, Brené Brown has spent over a decade studying vulnerability, courage, worthiness, and shame. In her work, she often discusses how our fear of vulnerability can cause us to withdraw and hide from the world, which can prevent us from fully participating in our lives and relationships. She clarifies our predicament in her book, *The Gifts of Imperfection*.

"When we feel rejected or criticized, it's easy to fall into a pattern of withdrawing and avoiding interaction with others," Brown notes. "However, this retreat often reinforces feelings of shame and inadequacy and ultimately hinders our growth and development."[2]

Let's dig into our challenges with relationships by bringing awareness to our tendency to withdraw when people don't treat us the way we want to be treated. When we encounter what we perceive to be rejection in relationships, our ego's default settings take the wheel and point all of our attention to how *we* experience things. This causes us to prioritize our needs over the needs of others and take everything personally. Whether it's a friend showing up late for drinks, an unintentionally offensive comment by a loved one, or honest feedback in the workplace, we're constantly on guard for evidence that others don't see and value us for who we are.

As you can imagine, this can make relationships difficult. When we're fixated on getting our needs for affirmation and validation met, we're unable to recognize (or fully understand) the needs and perspectives of others. This keeps us from enjoying generative connections with people in our lives.

UNDERSTANDING OUR INNER ELEVATOR

To paint the picture of our tendency to go inward, I'm reminded of a story my friend George shared about an experience he had at a week-long meditation retreat.

After settling into meditation one afternoon, George visualized going inside his brain and body. He boarded an imaginary elevator that descended from his brain to his gut. Inside his head, his eyes looked like two oval windows and were the only sources of light shining against the back of his skull. Those windows became faint dots as the elevator descended, and he looked down with fear into his inner blackness. "I don't want to go any further," he recalls saying to himself.

The difference between most people, like George, and us is that we're not afraid of riding that elevator as low as it can go. We're fascinated by our inner experience and believe our interior world is a place of refuge.

I can imagine my own inner elevator descending to the ground floor and, as it grinds to a halt and the doors open, I enter a cavern with shelves covering the walls. On these shelves, I collect and protect all my favorite wounds, stories, and defense mechanisms. Here I can sit in the safety of my own shadows, gaze upon the totems from which I've fashioned meaning, and relish how I'm different as I wallow in my emotions and hide from the misunderstandings I endure in the outside world.

Does your inner elevator take you to similar depths when you want to escape the unsatisfying reality of your life? What's on the shelves lining the walls of your inner cave? Do you also return to moments that remind you of your separateness from others and nurture the theories you've created about how no one understands you? Ah yes, we can spend hours down there worshiping the idols our ego has constructed to prevent us from connecting with others and participating in our lives.

Wouldn't you like to know how we ended up this way? I'm sure you would. People like us love throwing more self-reflection at our problems. We're happy to fill pages of journals while listening to hours of earnest music. We believe if we just had a little more time to savor the suffering, we might finally understand why we are the way we are.

Well, don't pick up a pen to jot down more notes about your lonely life just yet. We've lingered long enough in the cave at the bottom of our inner elevators and have little to show for it. We've not learned how to see through our feelings—and certainly not moved closer to others—by over-identifying with our emotional experience. So it's time to do something different.

If we want better relationships, we must recognize the default behaviors we practice when relationships don't give us exactly what we want. We're going to have to cop to our outsized interest in ourselves and own our unwillingness to pay attention to the experiences and needs of others—and do something about it.

NOTE

1. Henry David Thoreau, "Where I Lived, and What I Lived For," in *Walden; or, Life in the Woods* (Boston: Ticknor and Fields, 1854).
2. Brené Brown, *The Gifts of Imperfection* (Hazeldon, 2010).

CHAPTER 8

Coming to Terms with Our Self-Interest

Think of someone in your life who is selfless, generous, and kind by design. Can you picture them?

I have a friend named Melanie whose waking thought must be, "How can I make everyone else's life better today?" When my wife and I are departing on a trip, Melanie insists on seeing us off with a note, gift, or surprise. During difficult seasons, she's the one to peek her head in the front door with a smile, stopping by for a quick hug or to drop off some coffee.

Do you know someone like Melanie? If it's not a selfless friend, maybe you have a coworker, boss, mentor, or neighbor who simply does their best to make most interactions about you. They're happy to listen to you share about your life and the challenges you may be facing. They're not burdened by the time it takes to connect with and understand you. Honestly, what a gift those people are.

And if we're being really honest, we're also sometimes annoyed by their generosity and goodness, right? How are we supposed to keep up with their selflessness? Embarrassing as it is to admit, we often wince when the kindness of others reminds us of our own selfishness. I'm ashamed of this, but it's true.

People like us tend to behave in the opposite way of those magnanimous folks. Our default is often to ignore the needs of others. We're not intentionally trying to be selfish, rude, or detached; we've just got these big feelings we're contending with all the time. Now, couple our feelings with a fear of not being seen. This causes us to focus even more on our experience and less on the experience of others, and we quietly resent everyone for failing to intuit that we're hurting and need all the attention they can give us. When we're overtaken by our emotions, we rarely have the energy or awareness to attend to anyone else.

We must come to realize that our attention on ourselves can look a lot like self-interest to those around us. We might feel as if we're practicing self-care, but our outward display of that care can come across as aloofness and indifference.

When spelled out on the page, I hope it's possible to see this big blind spot of ours with a bit of clarity and compassion. It makes sense that we often feel our needs aren't being met in relationships since our desire for affirmation is insatiable. But we've got to wake up because the reality is that our big intrapersonal demands often lead others to distance themselves from us.

This is so core to how we interact with others that we often don't realize we're hogging the microphone in our relationships. I say this not to make you feel ashamed but to provide the kind of helpful feedback people like us must learn to receive. You and I aren't worse than anyone else for being this way. We're hurting for love and acceptance and mistakenly believe it's being kept from us. We're doing the best we can to find wholeness and peace. We must learn, however, that we cannot find wholeness or peace by seeking to control interactions or aborting social situations all together when our needs aren't met.

So, without shame, let's move forward into awareness and acceptance. By paying close attention to our default style of interacting with others, we can learn to show up in relationships in a healthier, more selfless way.

Let's start by considering your first thoughts upon waking up. What are they? Perhaps they're something like those I've had:

- What does my coworker think about me?
- How could my mother have said that to me yesterday?
- If only my Amazon package would come in today, then I'd be happy.
- I don't want to go to that party—who will I talk to?
- Did I come on too strong to my current love interest?

- Everyone must be judging me for that mistake I made.
- Why can't I seem to find the motivation to get my work done?
- I'm tired—I don't feel like doing anything.
- I feel rejected by everyone.
- Why don't my friends ever reach out to get together?
- I'm not getting what I want out of my relationships.
- I feel lost and depressed—what can get me out of this funk?
- Why don't I have any clarity on who I am and what I want?
- I'm so frustrated with myself, I can't even do the things that matter to me.

Scan the list above once more. What does every bullet have in common?

Me, me, me.

Put another way, tough as it may be to take: Our challenges in relationships, work, and life in general arise from our deeply rooted and extreme self-interest. It's taken me a long time and a big dose of humility to finally accept this and how I might come across to others.

If you look back on your own story with honesty, I'm betting you can admit certain friends, family, or groups have come to expect you to direct conversations back toward yourself. They anticipate that you're going to make things about your experience, perspective, or need for validation. I'm certainly guilty of this.

I recall one Christmas break during college when I traveled home to spend the holiday with my family. On the first night, everyone is gathered around the dinner table—my dad, mom, and two brothers. Over dinner, I'm sharing stories from my first semester as a newly minted university man. When I pause to take a bite of food, my youngest brother Gavin, who was eight at the time, begins to share something with excitement, but quickly looks at my father, then me, and says, "Oh, never mind."

I look quizzically at my father, then Gavin, and invite him to continue. Gavin shakes his head. I prod him again to share, and he refuses. I ask why he's not willing to share, and my young brother looks into his lap as he reluctantly whispers. "Dad told me when Reagan comes home he likes to talk a lot, and he takes all the air out of the room," he sighs. "So just let him go on for as long as he needs to, or else he'll get his feelings hurt."

Ouch. That one stung.

It stung because it's 100 percent true.

Thankfully, "Reagan sucking the air out of the room" is now a joke we recall with laughter and fondness for young Gavin's innocence. But even today as my family—all grown now—gathers around a table, I have to be aware of my tendency to overshare or sulk if it doesn't seem I'm getting the attention I desire.

Yes, our unconscious need for validation and unchecked self-interest can be a burden on others and complicate our relationships.

If we remain unaware, we'll continue to lean on all the strategies our ego has developed to keep the focus on us. We'll muscle through the pain of feeling unseen and into a place of power by fighting to be recognized so we can get our needs for depth, meaning, affirmation, or connection met. Or we'll dampen the mood of any room; with our emotions on display, we know how to make everyone walk on eggshells. The unhealthy versions of ourselves will fight to be noticed by taking the attention (love, affirmation, acceptance) we believe has been denied, lost, or stolen from us.

This extreme self-interest might smack of superiority. Sometimes I find myself desperately clinging to the belief I'm better than others (like those boar-hunting dudes in college) because I'm deeper, more reflective, more thoughtful, or more intentional. But in reality, our self-interest is defensiveness. Even if we summon superiority to criticize or confront others, we're only hiding how inferior we actually feel.

When driven by a deep fear of inferiority, it's unlikely we'll give attention to anyone else. The greatest hindrance to our growth is not that we are irrevocably inferior but that we tend to prioritize seeking validation, which we think we haven't fully received, over connecting with others by moving toward them.

Researcher and educator Dr. Joe Dispenza says that where we place our attention is where we place our energy.

The more attention we place on our perceived unmet needs, the more we fail to realize the story of humanity is not all about us.

Take a moment to consider your daily experience. Think about how you might be prone to these actions:

- Focus on your own experience in a conversation instead of another's.
- Attend to your needs before the needs of others.
- Disingenuously meet the needs of others so you can get what you need.
- Take offense before understanding what someone really means.
- Obsess over what you think you need to be happy, complete, or fulfilled.
- Ruminate about how others don't understand or respect you.

We must learn to catch ourselves in the act of turning the focus toward us and come to realize it is not others but our own self-interest that is keeping us from feeling connected. To truly understand the weight of our self-interest, we need to explore in a bit more detail the effects of our tendency to focus exclusively on our needs in relationships.

CHAPTER 9

Owning the Effects of Our Emotions

It's a crisp morning, and I'm typing away at my keyboard working on this book. The air outside is clear, and looking out the living room window, I see the shadows of the trees—backlit by the sunrise—beginning to darken the fence. I feel like I'm making good progress and am grateful for the momentum.

My wife, Elle, walks through the living room with some coffee. As she passes by, I ask her to take a brief look at the direction things are going. She nods, sits down, and balances her coffee on the arm of the couch. What a gal. She always says yes to helping me with creative projects even though she's sure to experience defensiveness and emotional reactions to whatever feedback she provides. This happens more often than I care to admit.

True to form, some of her feedback on a particular passage doesn't sit well with me. I believe her suggestions take away from my unique voice. As I correct her, she smiles and lets me finish, then patiently offers, "This is a perfect example of what you need to make sure to include in the section on relationships."

"What is?" I say without a clue.

"How your emotions, feelings, internal narrative—whatever—affect others." She goes on to say it would be a shame to write these chapters on the internal emotional experience of people like me and *only* feature the internal emotional experience of people like me. "What about the rest of us?" she prompts.

Nearly all of our challenges in relationships, Elle reminds me, are caused by our unending navel gazing and joyriding down our internal elevators. It rarely dawns on us to even consider the impact of our way of being on others.

In an effort to increase our consideration of others and acquire more awareness for ourselves, let us follow Elle's advice. Let's witness the ways we affect others when we're unconscious of our ego's tendency to make exchanges all about us. I'll share a few vignettes from my own experience to reveal how much power our insecurities and unchecked emotions actually wield in our relationships.

NO SPACE FOR ANYONE ELSE'S EXPERIENCE

For many years, one of my favorite (read: unhelpful) games when having a disagreement with a colleague, friend, or family member was called, "But let me *also* share how this makes me feel."

It looks like this: Let's say a teammate at work and I are having an exchange in which they are sharing how I hurt their feelings. Instead of recognizing that they are hurt and choosing to attune to their needs, I'm more interested in letting them know how *they* also hurt *my* feelings or slighted me in some way. It's like my ego is whispering, *if they get to feel pain and be recognized for it, you deserve the same.*

I essentially overwhelm them with all of the things I feel as a result of what they just shared, rather than honor their experience. In an instant, the spotlight is off the message they wished to communicate and focused squarely on my needs. It's a great strategy for confusing one's opponents, but it doesn't work so well in fostering trusting relationships.

Just because we are inclined to have an emotional reaction to nearly anything anyone might tell us, that doesn't mean we are entitled to rob others of the ability to let us know when we've done something that affects them.

It's more gracious for us to see how we can unwittingly overtake interactions and work toward making space for others to freely share their experience, just as we desire the ability to do ourselves.

THE VULNERABILITY SNARE

Alex and I both take deep breaths and maintain eye contact longer than we usually do. I've just begun taking on professional coaching clients, and he's engaged my services for a few sessions.

As I finish sharing a story about a difficult time in my life to illustrate a point, it's now time to explore portions of Alex's story related to a challenge he's experiencing. He bravely charges into a tender moment from his past that he believes has shaped his perspective. I can tell he's plumbing the depths of his awareness because he's clenching his teeth and now won't break his gaze from the trash can in the corner of the room.

He takes more deep breaths as he finishes his account then exhales a sigh of relief. I make a few closing comments to tie some ideas together, then crack my knuckles and open up my laptop while asking him when he'd like to schedule our next session. We get another date on the books, and as we're packing our bags to head out, he says quietly but firmly, "You know, it took a lot for me to share what I just shared. Just a little feedback: It would have been nice if you acknowledged me for opening up like that."

I totally missed the mark on this one. You see, one of our superpowers is fearlessness when it comes to experiencing and expressing our emotions. We come from the land of languishing in our feelings and are at home opening up about our struggles and insecurities. But vulnerability is not always easy for others. This is why our desire to drag all conversations to the deep end can sometimes throw people off. Of course, our vulnerability can be a gift as well. I'm sure you've had an experience where your willingness to open up has given others permission to do the same.

It's key for us to be aware of both our strengths and our shortcomings. If we're not careful, we might jump at the chance to be honest about our experience but then feel less interested in listening to what someone else is going through. Sometimes our desire to be seen can overpower our willingness to see. When someone does open up, we must recognize they're placing trust in us and honor their movement in our direction.

We have a gift of navigating challenging waters and can learn to become compassionate cotravelers with folks also experiencing life's heaviness. But we need to watch leaving people out to sea when we open up yet fail to acknowledge the courage it takes for them to do the same.

TAKING EVERYTHING PERSONALLY

I'll admit it. I still get my feelings hurt if someone doesn't attend my birthday party. I do. I'm sensitive to subtle slights and can react poorly when people disappoint me. How about you?

Sure, everyone takes things personally from time to time; it's just that we tend to get our feelings hurt more than others—and that can be a strain on relationships.

My old roommate Fred and I used to work out together in the mornings at the local YMCA. To fit both of our schedules, we needed to be at the Y right at 5:30 a.m. when it opened. Fred agreed to this. He gave his word. Yet, three out of five days, Fred would roll up *at least* fifteen minutes late. Can you believe it?

He'd arrive at the gym to find me stomping on a treadmill for our warm-up. He'd catch the last few minutes on the treadmill next to me while I gave him the silent treatment. On our way to the weights, I'd find a way to hurl some insult toward him. This happened dozens of times during the years we lived together.

What must that have been like for Fred? It's not even 6 a.m., and here we are, presented with an opportunity to spend time together and talk about what's going on in our lives while we practice healthy habits, but I'm too busy taking his tardiness personally.

Yes, when one is as self-interested as me, they find a way to view the punctuality of others as a referendum on the value of the relationship. When we take everything *so* personally and make interactions with others *so* serious, we push people away and make them feel bad in the process.

How can we expect others to hang around when they're worried everything they do or say might be offensive to us?

FORCING AUTHENTICITY ALL THE TIME

Avery is one of my wife's and my closest friends. A few years ago when pipes burst and flooded our home, causing our landlord to terminate our lease, she and her husband, George, took us in for a few months. During that sweet season, we'd gather in their backyard for coffee by the fire many mornings before work. Often, Avery and I would end up connecting about our big emotional lives and how our similar tendencies affect our relationships with our spouses.

One morning, we're laughing about events that took place at a wedding Avery and George recently attended and how she navigates her interactions with his family. "I feel like I have to be someone different when I'm around them," she says as she sips her coffee. She goes on to say she just wants to be accepted for who she is, for them to ask her questions about her life and her point of view, but often she feels pressure to fit into the mold of who they want her to be.

"Sometimes I'm like, why don't I just totally reject their norms and be me? No more pretending, no more faking it—this is me. I hope you like it!" Avery almost shouts.

Oh boy, can I connect to this. I've had similar experiences with my in-laws. For the longest time, it felt like they didn't care about my personhood. Like they didn't want to know the real me. So instead of blending into their family dynamic, I chose to withdraw, disengage, and do my best to direct all small talk back toward what I deemed important to discuss. To them, I probably seemed really difficult to connect with.

People like you, me, and Avery value authenticity above all else. Underneath this is the deep fear we're not accepted for who we really are—so when it seems others aren't curious about our unique perspective or fail take interest in the things that matter to us, a rebellious urge rises up inside.

What if I told you that you and I will never—ever—be inauthentic? We are at no risk of losing our deep and emotional honesty. It's part of who we are. Accepting this might help us relax when we find ourselves in the midst of (what we deem to be) an inauthentic interaction. If we could learn to trust that others aren't actively dismissing our inherent value when they have a different way of holding conversations, asking questions, or interacting, might it be possible we'd find a way to connect?

PREDICTING PERSONAL REJECTION

By this point, I hope you can see how we're often overly attuned to what's missing. Even if we're in a pleasant season of life, we're more focused on the things that still disappoint. We spend valuable energy thinking about all of the negatives and rarely focus on the positives.

For example, as a keynote speaker when I feel insecure after wrapping up a speech, I'll sometimes instigate a critique of my performance because I predict negative feedback is imminent from others. I used to be in the practice of approaching the event organizer and, before allowing them to share any reaction to my speech, sheepishly say something self-critical, like, "Oh man, I went way long and I definitely should have shortened the story in the beginning. I think I lost the audience a bit." I'd then encourage them to share their disapproval of my work.

Because we're already down on ourselves, one of our coping mechanisms is to get out ahead of potential criticism or feedback from others by practicing introjection, which is essentially the opposite of projection.

Our deployment of introjection looks a lot like adopting negative thoughts about ourselves before others share (what we worry might be) their negative thoughts. It's the classic "I'm breaking up with you before you break up with me" maneuver. Better to believe we're rejectable and not be surprised than to hope for acceptance from others only to be let down—again.

For example, we might notice someone questioning our progress on a project, which we read as distrust. Instead of viewing their inquiry as a simple request for an update, we bypass reality and choose to believe we are not to be trusted. We then build an identity around being someone who is not trustworthy and let that poison our relationship with ourselves, others, and our work.

But all we're doing is cutting ourselves down, then burdening others with building us back up. Back to the public speaking example. On one occasion, a friendly event organizer smiled as I listed my faults and then gently said, "Reagan, let me give you a little hint: Your job is to make this really easy for me as an event planner by reminding me of how glad I am that I hired you—not to convince me you could have been better. That's more work for me."

Because I've already got a negative view of myself, my ego reflexively tries to beat others to the punch by cutting me down before they can. Then, the pressure's on the other party to either pile on the criticism or accept the responsibility of convincing me I'm not as bad as I think.

We've got to own how we process our fears and stop saddling others with the weight of our sense of defectiveness. Others are rarely so critical of our abilities, and we can overly burden our relationships by trying to elicit negative feedback from others because we expect they doubt our value as much as we do.

CAUSING OTHERS TO WALK ON EGGSHELLS

It's worth calling back to my moody demeanor at the dance hall where we began our journey together. One of the most common ways we affect our relationships is by allowing our internal experience to muddy the external experience we could be sharing with others. In my work with people like us, I've found that, 100 percent of the time, we report wielding an emotional power over our interactions with others; we've conditioned others to fear our reaction if things don't go how we want them to.

I was on the phone with my mom recently sharing some difficulties I was facing. When I finished talking, she was silent for a long time. Then, she cautiously responded by speaking very slowly, generally, and almost robotically. Initially this frustrated me. *Why can't she be more personal and loving?* I thought.

I shared this with Elle afterward, and she (also cautiously) asked me to consider how I might have conditioned my mother to fear saying the wrong thing, which might put me in a mood. If I'm being honest, I can recall instances in all of my relationships where I descended into a funk because what someone said didn't give me everything I wanted. Their response didn't meet my expectations.

By no means am I encouraging you to silence your honesty in trusted relationships. It's worth considering, however, that we can cause others to fear our reactions to just about everything. We can be more loving and generous by beginning to identify moments when we're tempted to shut down or get in a funk based on something done unintentionally by an individual in our lives—and offer them grace instead of grouchiness.

No doubt this chapter is a tough pill to swallow. It's not easy uncovering our blind spots in relationships. Still more difficult is recognizing that the very default behaviors our ego has convinced us are essential to our safety can keep us from creating safe and meaningful connections with others.

For many of us, our greatest stumbling block in relationships is that we don't believe others could ever love us for who we are. When we take a hard look at this false belief, we'll begin finding evidence that we are the ones pushing others away. We'll begin to see how simple it is to bring lightness to our relationships by accepting people are in our lives not out of pity, but because they want to be.

To achieve the growth we're after and the personal connections we desire, we'll explore in the next chapter how the quality of relationships is measured by our willingness to give what we wish to receive.

CHAPTER 10

Giving What We Desire to Receive

I worked with a coach a few years ago who asked me what I most desired to receive from others: empathy, wisdom, or direction. Without blinking I responded, "Empathy." I want to feel seen, heard, and understood for my unique experience.

He then asked me which I tend to offer others: empathy, wisdom, or direction.

"Direction," I responded quickly.

My coach went on to kindly point out how difficult it is for me to give the very thing I desire. I'm so focused on getting my needs met that I subconsciously believe I must direct everyone in my life so they'll behave in a way that suits me. I want them to provide the affirmation, validation, or control I think I need.

"Your growth," my coach patiently told me, "is dependent upon your ability to empathize with the experience of others instead of hogging all the empathy for yourself."

It's funny how we who care so much about being validated for our emotional states are so unwilling to affirm the emotional states of others. We mistakenly believe there's only so much empathy to go around and fear that if we don't get our needs met in social interactions, relationships, or the workplace, we'll go on being unseen forever.

That's not fair to anyone—including us!

How many opportunities for connection have we missed because we believe being understood and accepted for our authentic selves comes first in every interaction? I ask you to consider a new approach. In our choice to reject the ride down on our internal elevator, see our self-interest with clarity, and give others the understanding we desire, we learn that connecting with others isn't so difficult after all.

I think back to that college party I attended with Kevin. If you'll recall, I walked away from the conversation with those guys believing they didn't understand *me*. I never once considered they were trying to show me how to connect with *them* by talking about sports and killing wild boars—things they cared about.

By making an honest effort to understand another's point of view, you'll find the connection you're both seeking. You'll learn how to better care for others—and will more likely feel the love in return.

"People are always trying to show you how to love them," a mentor of mine often quotes his grandmother as saying. To show more compassion for others, she emphasizes, requires heeding others' cues. "When will you begin paying attention?" she encourages.

Who knows what connection I missed with those rowdy gentlemen at that college party because I refused to see where the conversation might lead? What belonging might I have experienced had I joyfully joined the exchange instead of attempting to steer it in the direction of my interests?

I've learned that the reason folks like you and I are unwilling to make room for the experiences and preferences of anyone else is because we fear we'll never get our turn. We believe deep down that no one is interested in our unique perspective, and this keeps us uninterested in doing the work of relating to others. We're already nervous about being overlooked, so we're extra vigilant about ensuring we get the microphone in conversations. For us to grow, however, we must move toward others and, for the moment, let our social needs take a backseat.

This is undoubtedly difficult for those of our ilk. But trust me when I say that the gift of quality relationships is the reward for passing on opportunities to control interactions in order to get the cheap attention we think we need.

If that doesn't sound difficult enough, let me tighten the screw one more turn. (Remember, this is for our own good.) It is true that the connection, acceptance, validation, reassurance, belonging, recognition, and relationships we desire will show up (sometimes quickly, sometimes slowly) when we are willing to freely give our energy to be there for others. This absolutely will happen over time. But we must prepare ourselves for the reality that our relationships with others won't always have the depth, vulnerability, or authenticity we believe all worthwhile relationships should contain. Simply put, sometimes we might be disappointed in the return on our investment. Yes, the connection with others, for which we are learning to so diligently silence our egos, might not be the kind of connection we initially desired.

In our old lives, this truth could reaffirm our belief that no one will ever understand us or meet our needs. This kind of relational "miss" might even deepen the judgments we hold about most people's failure to be authentic or intentional.

But that's not who we are anymore. We're now waking up and choosing to believe that sometimes one just makes friends with a person at a party by talking about hot water heaters. We're not always supposed to be teeing up a deep conversation. Most relationships take time, a willingness to give away the kind of attention you desire, and a belief the other party is honestly trying to interact with you in the best way they know how.

WHY FINDING "YOUR PEOPLE" ISN'T THE CURE-ALL

At this point you might be thinking: *So what's the problem? I'll just postpone investing in relationships until I can find a collection of introspective, deep people, and then I'll be set. No more shallow small talk for me, thank you!*

Yes, this is an option. With determination and discernment, perhaps you could fashion your very own troupe of melancholy souls who join together in the holy and endless exploration of the meaning of life. But creating a social circle comprised only of people who give you what you think you need isn't the path of growth we're after. At worst, it's a shortcut to another dead end—the kind of enticing alternate path that allows you to go deeper inside yourself but nowhere else. And let's not forget, people like me and you are highly skilled at spotting what's missing in our lives and relationships. Even if we did form the perfect all-star team of deep and wounded companions, we'd eventually find ways to blame them all for not adequately meeting our unpredictable needs and expectations.

Our growth in relationships is about learning to take the focus off of ourselves by meeting the relational needs of others. Putting others first with an honest heart is our path to freedom from our fear of people, the deeply held belief we are misunderstood, and the urge to thoughtlessly assign judgment to those who prefer to connect in different ways.

"The number-one thing we can do to improve the health of our relationships is work on ourselves," my wife, Elle, tells clients when teaching her Enneagram course for couples.

This phase of our journey where we address our challenges with relationships must be about more than finding the "right" relationships so we no longer suffer the pains of being misunderstood. We must objectively witness our own avoidance of people and situations we worry might wound us. We must balance our need for self-protection with our desire for growth—caring for ourselves while boldly moving ahead to make progress in our lives and relationships.

It is worth remembering that our ego will attempt to trap us into thinking that we can only do one or the other:

protect ourselves or grow. But this kind of dualistic think-ing will ultimate inhibit both. We have to trust that taking care of ourselves and being selfless with others are not mutu-ally exclusive. Exiting our internal world and venturing into the unknown territory of relationships is our path toward freedom, and we'll only realize this true freedom when we recognize there is no finite amount of love, acceptance, and attention in relationships.

"The stronger the ego, the stronger the sense of separ-ateness between people," author and teacher Eckhart Tolle reminds us. "The only actions that do not cause opposing reactions are those that are aimed at the good of all. They are inclusive, not exclusive. They join; they don't separate."[1]

It's probably appropriate at this point to address possible objections to the idea of balancing meeting our needs with prioritizing the needs of others. If you follow any Instagram psychologist, you've likely read plenty of posts (particularly around the holidays) about protecting your boundaries and making sure you don't lose yourself in service of others. It seems like every other post is focused on prioritizing our own self-care by not allowing toxic people or unhealthy rela-tionships to drain us of our sanity and self-worth.

I certainly agree we must be vigilant about ensuring we're not damaged by relationships with unsafe people. I'd also argue our work here goes a step further than protect-ing ourselves, as our ego has tried to do without avail for years. We are in pursuit of transformation. This book is not for everyone—those with people-pleasing tendencies, for instance, should heed different advice. But if it is for you,

I'm here to confirm that healthier, more substantive relationships come from selflessness rather than self-imposed protection. Everyone has a shadow they're contending with; our shadow is not characterized by giving too much but by giving too little.

CONNECTION COMES FROM CURIOSITY

At this point, if you're still set on clinging to the identity of the lonely traveler and faulting others for difficulties you encounter in relationships, then this is as far as we can journey together.

On the other hand, if you're ready to continue dismantling the old perspectives preventing you from finding the acceptance you desperately desire, let's keep going. Here are a few questions we must contend with to foster deeper connection with others:

- Is it possible others are just as interested in getting their relational needs met?
- Are they really actively ignoring, misunderstanding, or denying me attention or validation?
- Might they instead be trying to be seen, heard, and understood as well?
- What would happen if I met their needs instead of focusing on mine?

I want you to notice something about the spirit of these questions. They're rooted in willing curiosity. They invite the possibility that our ego might not actually know what's best for us.

A friend of mine is fond of ending any assumption about his life circumstances with the phrase "or not." When he feels stressed because his daughter had a meltdown and needs to talk on the phone for an hour during the workday, he might quip, "So, now I'll be behind on work and have to stay up late, which will probably mean I drop the ball on something else . . . or not."

We must similarly wrestle with our errant assumptions about what's best for us and others and understand that these two things aren't necessarily mutually exclusive. We have to see our unconscious self-interest and admit that we actually aren't the best judges of what will make us happy in relationships. Our life stories and complicated relationships to this point should confirm this. A better behavior moving forward is to approach interactions with curiosity about the needs of others, a willingness to give what we wish to receive, and the courage to say to ourselves, "or not," when our ego screams for us to make interactions about ourselves.

We must never forget the age-old wisdom that we receive what we're looking for when we first choose to give it. The internal elevator can wait. When we attend to others in our lives, we'll find the same care we're seeking and learn that relationships aren't (always) as complicated as they seem.

Good work so far. Now that we've brought awareness to our challenges in relationships—and before that, our challenges with work—it's time to uncover the root cause of our pain.

It's time to better understand our relationship with ourselves.

NOTE

1.   Eckhart Tolle, *A New Earth* (New York: Dutton, 2005).

CHAPTER 11

What's Wrong with Me?

It's day one of first grade, and I walk down the hallway to my classroom sporting big Coke-bottle glasses with Donald Duck's face on each side. My eyes are magnified by about three times, making me look like Martin Scorsese's bastard Welsh son. The school smells like sharpened pencils and cleaning solution, and I'm desperate for belonging.

Earlier that morning, over breakfast, I told my father I had a strategy for making friends. Every day as we put our backpacks in our cubbies, I'm going to approach a new class-mate and say with a smile, "Hi, I'm Reagan. Do you want to be my friend?"

My father smiles almost tearfully and says, "I think that's a really good idea, son."

But it's not so easy. The first kid I approach says, "Don't be weird, Donald Duck."

First graders are mean.

One day during PE, a kid named Robert grabs two hula hoops, holds them up to his face, and shouts, "Hey! I'm Reagan!"

All the kids laugh, call me four-eyes, and ask me if I can see through walls. Quietly, in that moment, the seed of my deep sense of defectiveness is planted.

Thankfully, as the weeks go on, I'm able to make a few friends. One of them is Lucas, who has hair like Jonathan Taylor Thomas. He's tan and so cool he eats a vegetarian diet already. He'll probably live forever. Every day at recess, a pack of girls strap their jellies on tight and chase Lucas around the playground. He's like Elvis or something.

On one particular sunny afternoon, Lucas and I are playing four square when, in the distance, a squealing horde of bouncing bows forms like a gathering storm and barrels toward us. He looks at me with a self-assured smile and sprints off the paved basketball court down a hill toward the soccer fields. I smile back with squinted eyes big as trash can lids and follow suit.

For a moment, it seems the girls are chasing both of us—and I feel something like confidence. As I match Lucas's stride, I begin to wonder, *What will happen if they catch us? Will we just stand there unsure of what to do next because we haven't played out the rest of this game?*

The foot chase continues until we reach the end of the field and (when I recall this moment, I see it from above) Lucas peels off to the right and I unknowingly cut left. From the sky, I imagine it looks like a *Planet Earth* episode about a herd of antelope following their leader to a predestined location. Only there's one antelope who follows a false scent and ends up lost for months, finally collapsing to the ground. Wind whips its notched ears as flies slip on the surface of its unmoving eyeballs.

"Lost, separated from the herd, the misguided beast dies alone," David Attenborough narrates.

But long before this moment—looking back as it trotted in the wrong direction—the antelope knew no one was behind him. Only a cloud of dust in the herd's wake. That is the real death.

"This lonely calf belongs now to the wind," Attenborough intones dispassionately. "There will be but one shadow cast across the barren landscape on its final journey."

That's me: a boy with glasses too heavy for his face, looking over his shoulder. I'm squinting with one eye at Lucas leading all those fine ladies to the water fountain of inclusion. It seems clear they're all going to grow up knowing how to date one another, read signals from the opposite sex, and participate in the dance of love. As I catch my breath with my hands on my knees all alone on the wrong side of the playground, I start to think something might be wrong with me.

OVERLY ATTUNED TO WHAT'S MISSING

Elle and I are out on an afternoon walk in our East Austin neighborhood with our white Labrador, Lily. It's a sunny March day, and as we talk about work and friends, we end up having a tangential conversation about the differences in how we each see the world.

Elle tends to be more hopeful in her assessments while I focus mostly on what's lacking. We pass by a flower bed that's overgrown and unkempt. "Geez, this place needs a haircut," I say, seeing but not really appreciating the explosion of color bursting from the soil. "Don't they have groundskeepers to take care of this trail?"

Elle laughs and smiles. I ask her what she's laughing about, and she says, "I was just thinking how beautiful spring is. There are reminders of new life everywhere."

Later, as we're planning our wedding, I can't focus on all the guests who RSVP'd "yes" to travel to North Carolina for our nuptials. Instead, I lament about those not coming. *Do they not value our relationship?* I wonder.

When my mom calls to ask with interest about how work is going, I find it difficult to celebrate my full travel schedule or that I'm speaking on bigger stages, or, hell, the fact I'm doing what I always dreamed of doing. I'm more likely to focus on my fear that my speeches are too varied in their subject matter. *If I was a better professional speaker, I'd have more streamlined speaking topics*, I complain.

Please understand that it is not my intent to portray people like you and me as wrong, negative, or depressing. Instead, I want to nudge us toward a more positive view of ourselves rooted in awareness and acceptance. In order to cultivate that self-acceptance, we must practice being truthful with ourselves. We must observe how we behave and who we've become—not with shame but compassionate objectivity. Awareness is our path to freedom, so let us now choose to see with clarity our tendency to focus on what's missing—and how this starts with the way in which we view ourselves.

When someone you know and trust asks how you're doing, what is your typical response? Even on a good day, do you share what's going well, or do you tend to talk about what's lacking? On an afternoon when you choose to relax and take a break, is it with a spirit of gratitude for the chance to recharge, or do you feel a tinge of shame? Do you wonder if there's something wrong with you because you're not as productive as others?

When thinking about your career, relationships, where you live, what you look like, or where your life seems to be headed, is your view rosy or dim?

Have you ever looked back on a job you disliked and believed didn't align with your passions, only to realize it was actually a pretty good gig? Might you now be focused on everything wrong with your vocational trajectory instead of seeing that you're doing a little better than you were six months ago?

As we previously discussed, have you abandoned friendships because, no matter how hard someone tried, you always found fault in the relationship?

Now let's shift to how you see yourself in those quiet, reflective moments.

Are you compassionate with yourself, and do you have a hopeful view of your future? When you make mistakes, do you give yourself grace? Are you able to summon confidence in your abilities when it's time to participate and trust that you'll get better over time? Can you see yourself as an equal in relationships with others?

Or have you given up on your chances at fulfillment, love, and peace as I did most of my youth and young adulthood? Do you miss the richness of relationships because you secretly wonder why anyone would want to be in a relationship with you? Quietly, do you wonder whether you've got anything to offer at all?

You might argue that everyone is hard on themselves. Consider the impossible standards set for us today and upheld by social media. Maybe you accept feeling down or even occasionally battling depression as a natural consequence for not measuring up. *Welcome to a Westernized world where performance is king and everyone feels a little inadequate!*

But it's more than that.

If you're anything like me, you've moved past the temporary sadness of feeling "less than." You're not just experiencing momentary discomfort while you find your place in a new job, school, or social setting. Instead, you've settled at the bottom of your internal elevator with a numb and quiet belief—paradoxically, almost a spirit of confidence—in your unworthiness.

Ah, yes. This is what we've been digging for.

We've recognized how we mistake our feelings—big emotions—for reality. By exploring our confusing relationship with motivation at work and acknowledging our extreme self-interest in relationships, we have come to realize our difficulty with life is ultimately rooted in our deep sense of defectiveness.

All of our challenges stem from our belief that we are unwhole—or, at best, that we were made with spare parts. We believe we're missing the necessary ingredients to be a normal person. Of course we struggle with motivation when we're certain we don't possess the knowledge and skills to adequately participate in life (or the ability to acquire them).

It makes perfect sense that we struggle to feel seen in relationships since we don't believe we deserve to be seen. We fight to meet our needs through self-interest or withdraw when we feel overlooked because we've come to trust the story that we're not worth anyone's time. Our life experience reflects the way we view ourselves.

"We do not see things as they are," as writer Anaïs Nin puts it. "We see them as we are."[1]

When you're missing what you believe you need to be whole, the entire world comes up short. This is the root cause of our shame, moodiness, reluctance to dance, and fear of taking action. Bringing awareness and acceptance to our core wound of defectiveness will guide us to a new way of being. But first, we must address the stumbling blocks we've encountered along the way.

NOTE

1. Anaïs Nin, *Seduction of the Minotaur* (Chicago: The Swallow Press, 1961), 124.

CHAPTER 12

Coming to Terms with Our Need for Acceptance

The insecurity I first developed on the playground in elementary school—the unconscious narrative that I'm somehow defective—is hardwired into my brain by the time I reach middle school, and I still carry it with me as I navigate high school. Seeking to compensate for my sense of inadequacy, I try to blend in and gain the approval of my peers.

Around sophomore or junior year, I develop a monthly practice of assessing how classmates view me. I solemnly close the door to my bedroom, pull out my yearbook, and flip through each page, putting a check mark on the pictures of people I believe see me in a positive light. The photos without check marks become my to-do list. Each week I try to amass more check marks by making it a point to say hello to or sit at lunch with someone new. Given that there's 627 students in my class, this is no small task.

All I think about is what other people think about me. Do they accept me? Would they speak kindly of me? At the end of each school year, I measure the quality of those two semesters by the amount of check marks I amass. I don't know it yet, but I'm on a daily search for evidence that I'm not defective. It all started in elementary school, when I came to believe I was an undesirable who couldn't fit in socially. These doubts in my potential, my intelligence, my athleticism, and ultimately, my worth, echoed into the rest of my life.

This negative perception of myself continued to snowball after high school. Reagan in his twenties was resentful, unfulfilled in work, a self-interested friend, unable to maintain healthy romantic relationships, and an active alcoholic. Everything I did was artfully designed to help me fit in, find love, and fast-track myself professionally. I thought I could quiet the voices of inadequacy if only I acquired those external indicators of success. Not one thing I did came from a place of honest desire, generosity, or inner peace. I criticized myself for trying too hard and in the same breath berated myself for not trying hard enough.

I drank about all of this and grew more resentful of people who seemed less concerned about doing things "correctly," which had become my obsession. To manage my fear of being singled out as inadequate, I carefully planned my life around the behaviors and activities I thought were necessary to fit in and kept an unforgiving tally of what I was doing right or wrong. Over time, I developed a quiet satisfaction when others, too, couldn't seem to do life right. I felt more in control when I judged people's worth or criticized their performance. I believed they were doing it to me, so why not beat them to the punch? If I felt defective, I'd sure as hell make sure everyone else shared the same classification.

Years of doing this pulls one away from actually living. I was the wallflower, mumbling about the missteps of the people on the dance floor, jealous of their confidence but suspect of their motives. I was critical of others' sense of community and desperate to know what it felt like to participate without fear. I kept people at arm's length because I didn't want them to get too close and learn how disappointing I actually was. I worked long hours doing things I didn't care about to demonstrate to others I could hang. I drank myself stupid most nights of the week. Some mornings, while looking in the mirror, I'd whimper to my reflection about how tired I was of whatever game I was playing.

This strategy of manipulating others into validating me because I couldn't validate myself was not going as planned.

A SENSE OF UNWORTHINESS LEADS TO RESENTMENT

Finally, I admit to myself that I need to stop drinking. On a cold and rainy night, I pace outside of an unfriendly looking building on a poorly lit street corner before walking into an Alcoholics Anonymous meeting. Shortly after, a sponsor begins to guide me through AA's twelve steps of recovery.

Steps four and five are tough ones for most folks in AA. You have to write down all of your resentments and fears and talk with your sponsor about the harm you've done to others. This is the first time most of us have owned up to the behaviors we excused while we were in active addiction.

While working through step five, I sit down with my sponsor to go over a list of everyone I resent. This is basically everyone I've ever known. We tick through each of the names on my list, a process similar to, but the opposite of, my high school yearbook practice. Instead of wanting everyone on the page to like me, I've come to resent them for not liking me enough. I've scrawled comments explaining why I resent each person on the list: They're too obsessed with things like how they look, what others think, their job, or their workout routine. I think everyone is overly focused on something in their lives that doesn't really matter. Unconsciously, I resent them for putting their time and energy toward anything but helping me feel better about myself.

My sponsor looks at me with understanding after I've read through all the names and shared my rationale for resenting each person.

"Reagan, it is not all of these people who are obsessed with the wrong things. You're obsessed with these people. They're living their lives, maybe committing some of the crimes you're charging them with—but you have no idea what's going on in their heads," he tells me. "Perhaps they've found a way to do something that brings them fulfillment. Meanwhile, you're missing out on living your own life. You're spending your energy judging how others are living theirs and resenting them for not giving you the affirmation you need to learn how to give yourself."

I'm silent for a long moment. He suggests we take a break. We quietly shuffle around his house, visit the bees he keeps in the backyard, pour ourselves a couple cups of coffee, and sit down to continue the work. He revisits my list of resentments as his bees buzz in the side yard. After a spell, he looks at me over his glasses. "Ah, there's a resentment missing here," he says.

I take the page and review every family member, friend, coworker, acquaintance, and person I follow on Instagram, and assure him, "No, I *literally* think that's everyone."

"What about you?" he asks, handing the list back to me.

I look over the page again searching for my name, though I know I won't find it.

He continues. "What if I suggested the root of so many of these resentments—hell, the root of your drinking—is largely a result of your deep resentment for yourself and lack of acceptance for who you are?"

RECOVERING FROM OUR SENSE OF DEFECTIVENESS

For me, this is the miracle of recovery. I realize this whole time I've been drinking about not receiving the acceptance and validation I want to feel, and the emotions of sadness and melancholy I feel as a result. My true addiction is to an identity of defectiveness, a personality rooted in victimhood, and the activities that numb all the feelings I can't manage. As they say in AA, my drinking was but a symptom.

Author Shauna Niequist describes our need to recover the wholeness of who we've always been, rather than looking for what's missing, in her book *Present Over Perfect.*

"I thought it would be about leaving behind the expectations and encumbrances of the past. It is," she writes of her experience while navigating a challenging season in her life. "What I didn't know is that it would feel so much like recovering an essential self, not like discovering a new one."[1]

What I'm really doing—when I'm tangled in my emotions and think they represent reality, when I doubt my ability to participate, when I obsess over my point of view or think everyone is out to get me—is avoiding the work of recovery. I'm putting my energy toward reminding myself of who I'm not instead of recovering the wholeness that belonged to first-grade Reagan before he developed a false narrative about his unworthiness.

The same goes for you.

In no way am I saying that if you identify with the stories I've laid out that you must have a substance abuse issue. But I do believe we're all in some stage of recovery from something. For us, it's recovering from our obsession with, or addiction to, the idea that we don't measure up to anyone else and the maladaptive ways we cope.

Father Richard Rohr captures this beautifully in his book *Breathing Under Water: Spirituality and the Twelve Steps.*

"We are all spiritually powerless . . . not just those physically addicted to a substance," Rohr contends. "Alcoholics just have their powerlessness visible for all to see. The rest of us disguise it in different ways and overcompensate for our more hidden and subtle addictions and attachments, especially our addiction to our way of thinking."[2]

It's time to cast off the belief that we are unwhole and recover the equanimity that allows us to experience life's joys, connect with others, and face new challenges every day. Every person has their own path to growth. Our particular burden involves learning to believe we're OK, we're normal, and that there's nothing wrong with us. Our work is to surrender our desire for emotional control and, to borrow another saying from AA, accept life on life's terms.

Now we're at another inflection point. Since starting this journey, we've brought awareness to how we:

- Experience outsized emotions that we mistake for reality.
- Let our cloud of feelings prevent us from participating in work and life.
- Sabotage ourselves in professional pursuits because we fear feedback or criticism.
- Build elaborate internal lives, and draw inward in the face of outward challenges.
- Default to self-interest in order to get our needs met in relationships.

We now must admit that our overly sensitive demeanor and obsession with our internal experience stem from having a deep, unconscious conviction that we're broken beyond repair. And this is as far as most people like us make it.

Most people like us know they're emotional and might admit they're a tad self-referencing. They sense a deep lack in themselves but remain stuck in the loop of feelings, isolation, and shame instead of considering they might not be as defective as they mistakenly believe.

But you and me, we can break the cycle.

NOTES

1. Shauna Niequist, *Present Over Perfect* (Zondervan, 2016).
2. Richard Rohr, *Breathing Under Water: Spirituality and the Twelve Steps* (2011).

CHAPTER 13

The Curse of Comparison

Do you ever feel like you've failed before you even get out of bed? Mornings can be hard for folks like us. When the alarm sounds for the second or third time after I've hit snooze and I scramble in shame to start my day, I wonder if anyone else also snoozes their alarm. *Am I the only sorry excuse of a person who can't wake up today?*

After this, I'll start worrying about my relationships with everyone who is attending my first meeting of the day. I haven't finished that update I was supposed to complete for the meeting—and I fear everyone knows it.

In the shower, I practice a couple conversations I might have with people who I fear are silently judging me, just in case. Before the hot water runs out, I perfect the quips I'm going to use, and I imagine whatever negative thing people think about me will be reversed after I tell them what I rehearsed.

This is a lot of energy to expend before 9 a.m., a heavy way to start the day. But folks like us, when unconscious, can obsess about how we stack up. We wake consumed by a spirit of self-loathing and comparison.

Our ability to simply begin our day is thwarted because we've disconnected ourselves from reality and overestimated our own importance by fantasizing about how unimportant others must think we are. You can imagine how one's day is going to go when their first waking thoughts are centered around not only their own defectiveness but also the idea that everyone else is in on the joke.

To truly find peace, we must take on our preoccupation with standing and status. We emotional types tend to see life through the lens of relationships. Even if you're a loner, it's likely you spend an inordinate amount of time considering your life in relation to others. Our obsession with what others think about us is so common there's a name for it: spotlight effect. The concept refers to our egocentric belief that we're being noticed more than we really are.

In a classic study on the spotlight effect, researchers gave participants a T-shirt featuring a potentially embarrassing image or message. Before sporting their new shirt in public places, they were asked to estimate how many people might notice or remember the shirt. Participants consistently overestimated the number of people who actually would take notice of their quirky clothing, according to study's results published in the *Journal of Personality and Social Psychology.*[1]

For us emotional folks, we believe even our private experiences are visible to everyone else. We think our sense of inferiority, extreme self-criticism, and overwhelming doubt are not only witnessed by others but factor into their perception of us. We imagine everyone else has access to the negative narratives that run our lives.

Remember the movie *The Truman Show* with Jim Carrey? He plays Truman Burbank, who is unknowingly the subject of the most popular television show in the world. From birth, every second of his life—his private experiences and most intimate moments—are captured on camera for the entire world to see.

Have you ever wondered if you're on "The Truman Show"? Be honest. I know I have.

But don't worry; you're not alone. You're not an outsider because you think this way, so allow yourself to relax and bring awareness to how comparison shows up in our lives.

My particular obsession with comparison looks like this:

- When I'm performing at my worst and just can't get it together, I fear everyone knows it.
- I think others are privy to my private ambitions and find it humorous that I believe I'm capable of reaching my goals.
- Sometimes I worry that people remember the mistakes I've made—forever—even if I had good intentions.
- On days I take time for myself or try something out of the box, I fear that colleagues have a sixth sense and intuitively know I'm slacking or wasting time.

- I'm convinced everyone is paying close attention to my missteps and regularly thinks about whether or not I have what it takes.
- I pray for the day that I'll finally understand everyone's expectations of me and learn all the rules; then, I think, I'll be able to do everything right and avoid criticism.
- I'm fairly certain all the people in my life convene on a regular basis to discuss how unimpressive, emotional, and misguided I am.

Ultimately, so much of this comes down to our deep desire to do life right. We're terrified of doing things wrong and being shamed for it, which would confirm our belief that we we're broken from the start. But we must remember that the criticism we experience comes from within, as does the constant game of comparison.

Everyone isn't fixated on our inadequacies, as we've erroneously come to believe. When you shift your thinking and begin to see that you're not uniquely incomplete, you'll slowly cease projecting your fears on everyone else. Then things will really begin to change.

NOTE

1. Gilovich, T., Medvec, V. H., & Savitsky, K. (2000). "The spotlight effect in social judgment: An egocentric bias in estimates of the salience of one's own actions and appearance," *Journal of Personality and Social Psychology* 78(2), 211–222.

CHAPTER 14

Changing Our Perception of Ourselves

Shortly after starting my own business as a speaker and facilitator, I got invited to a big board room on the top floor of an Austin high rise. I'm here to pitch a private equity firm on a series of workshops I've developed.

But immediately upon exiting the elevator, as my sneakers squeak across the marble floor to the receptionist's desk, I fall into self-loathing. I hate myself. I'm underdressed and feel underprepared. I peer into the glass-walled room where the meeting will take place and see more people around the table than printouts I have in hand.

Oh boy, you're way out of your league, Reagan, I tell myself.

I interpret the receptionist's disinterest in small talk as a judgment of me, my clothes, and my business acumen. I imagine she's laughing inside and hoping for my failure. But I beat her to the punch because I already believe I'm a failure (introjection at work). In this moment, I can feel myself beginning to board my inner elevator. I want to retreat down to the safety of my cave where I have plenty of stories on the shelf about my inadequacies as a salesperson. But I'm learning to notice what's happening, so I take a seat in the lobby and breathe for a moment, feeling the sturdy arms of the chair. I plant my feet on the floor and consider what her world might look like, what deadlines she's under, and that she might just be a shy person.

Upon being summoned to the boardroom, I shake hands, make a joke about sharing printouts to save trees, and think to myself, *What if you just participated in this meeting as if nothing is wrong?* I manage, with some difficulty, to quell my feelings of inadequacy and stay in the real world. I paint a big, imaginative picture of the workshops I'd deliver if we partnered together. I field their questions as best I can and am honest in acknowledging when I don't have the answers.

The meeting continues, and I start to get frustrated because they aren't as excited as I want them to be. I see a few smiles, but they only buy into part of my vision— saying no to a few of the ideas I'm really excited about. One guy looks at his phone the whole time. The meeting wraps quickly—*too quickly*, I worry.

As I ride the elevator down to the parking garage, I also go down my inner elevator. I think about all the things the people in the boardroom didn't give me. I'm worried about how unimpressed they seemed. *They'll never call me*, I whisper to my reflection in the elevator doors.

Several weeks later, I still haven't heard from them. My greatest fears are confirmed. One morning in a burst of bravery, I go for a walk around the block and call my contact at the private equity firm to inquire about their decision.

I pass a chain-link fence enclosing a Rottweiler who begins stalking me, smelling the air for my blood. We make eye contact. She unleashes a vicious string of barks that push me off the sidewalk and into the street. As I make the corner, I see a chicken coop in the same yard. The black-and-brown barking beast loses interest in me and saunters over to a hen, which she sniffs and nudges with her snout. The Rottweiler then lays down amidst the clucking mothers.

"Hello? Reagan?" I hear on the other end of the phone.

"Hey, Reagan, we're sorry for the delay. Things are crazy with this acquisition. We're swamped. We'd love to go with you. Your approach seems different and less Microsoft-y than the person we normally use. Can we get some dates on the calendar?"

We schedule the workshop, and I hang up the phone, still standing in the street next to the scary-looking dog I thought didn't want me around. Then, the Rottweiler gets up, trots over to the fence, sits on her haunches, and parts her teeth to pant in the warming afternoon. She almost manages a smile before her owner comes out with a garbage bag and waves.

"Lucy, have you made a new friend?" he asks the dog as he drops the black bag into the garbage bin. "She's a worthless guard dog. These chickens could kill her if they ever conspired to." He laughs and walks back inside.

There I remain in thought for some time. My ego is working hard to hang on to this notion that I'm an intruder in this dog's domain and it wants to kill me. I'm also cling-ing to the narrative that no one wants to do business with me when they don't bend over backward to affirm me from the get-go. I slowly accept the truth that maybe the world's not against me.

I'm just one of those chickens on a warm afternoon wad-dling around a one-hundred-pound dog whose chief con-cern is sniffing out the best patch of shade for a nap. I'm just a guy with professional services some people might want and some people may not. There's no organized group of folks opposing my efforts. There's no mystical force at odds with my attempts to get what I want out of life.

Perhaps there's nothing wrong with me at all.

CHAPTER 15

Not So Broken After All

It's moving day.

I'm leaving the house I own with my mentor and boss. We purchased it a few years ago and transformed the downstairs into a coworking space for employees of his consulting firm. I'm now cashing out my portion and starting anew. I have no job and no significant other, and I'm going on sabbatical so I can figure out the rest of my life.

I'm still a year or two away from my drinking nearly taking me out. I'm oblivious to my real issues and just grateful to throw all of my energy into the fantasy of three months off. The doorbell rings. The movers have arrived. I breathe in and out.

The movers make quick work of loading up my limited possessions. I watch as if I'm observing my life from the outside and seeing pieces of it carried off. I wonder why it seems so easy to relocate my physical belongings yet so difficult to reorder and purge the emotions I carry with me. When the movers pick up the bed and haul it down the stairs, there are a few things left underneath: a beat-up guitar pick and a card from my old manager, Laura.

Laura carried me for a season when I couldn't carry myself. For years, we had weekly calls that turned into therapy sessions. I'd complain about my love life, lament about how others treated me, and moan about my lack of clarity or direction. She patiently listened and offered support. She tried to tell me a more positive story about myself that I was unable to believe at the time. I open Laura's card and sit in the rectangle where my bed had been, the carpet worn down by tubs of old journals I'd once kept beneath the box springs.

"Great job planning the firm's annual conference—again," she'd written in her kindly script. *"You showed us how to believe in magic—now I hope you'll believe in your own magic."*

I sit there until the movers finish packing my things. For a moment, I look back on all the memories in that home with lightness. I believe others are for me and I'm not defective. *I can make a contribution that matters*, I think. *I simply need to show up and participate.* I feel for the first time in a long time that I am simply OK.

Sometimes others carry us. I hope you've had people in your life who recognized and named the best in you when all you could do was wallow in self-loathing. Laura is one of many who helped me see what I refused to see about myself.

Friends can have a tremendous, positive impact on our lives if we let them. Yet ultimately you and I must still make the choice to accept a different narrative about who we are. We must change our beliefs about our worthiness and accept that maybe we have what it takes to live the meaningful life we've always wanted.

We're the only ones who can give ourselves permission.

THE MOST IMPORTANT DECISION YOU'LL EVER MAKE

Here's a radical proposal: You can base the whole way you live on a lie (like, say, that you're defective). Or, you can make the big jump with me and—despite the fight your ego is going put up—decide to believe the opposite. You can accept that there's nothing wrong with you.

I understand if your first instinct is to reject this proposal outright. I did that for years.

I mean, even if you relate to the themes covered so far, maybe I didn't quite articulate your particular disposition with 100 percent accuracy. *You don't know my full story,* you might still be thinking. And you're right.

I don't know what you've been through. You may be a white-collar mope with a decent job you hate, or you could have no work and no prospects. You might be blessed with patient relationships and have people who love you despite your moodiness, or perhaps you've never had one true friend. Maybe you've learned how to navigate social situations—or it's possible you can't interact with others to save your life.

Your parents could have raised you wrong, and you might have failed at every single thing you've ever tried. Maybe it's even sadder than all that.

I don't know your story, but I do know what it's like to feel like an outsider who can't seem to figure out the right way to do life. I know what it's like to feel alone and unwell. Accordingly, this is the part where I try to convince you that there's hope and let you know you're not as defective or broken as you may have believed. But because I'm like you, I have a sneaking suspicion that you might be hesitant to grab my outstretched hand. By the way, it's your ego that's suspicious. Remember, your ego feels safe in the world it's constructed where you're a victim and the broken, disappointing minor character of your life. It's your ego—not your true self—that is afraid to release the negative stories about your worth.

I only ask you to pay more attention to our similarities than our differences. Have you felt seen in some way on our journey together? If so, might that indicate that you are not alone?

Finally—is it possible for you to consider, even for a moment, that you are not as uniquely defective as you once thought? That's all it takes. Just a willingness to believe you are not broken.

No, you're not broken; you're just human.

I've coached many people like you and me who were convinced that something was inherently wrong with them. But their perspective changed when they made a decision to stop believing the lie and start acting like they were OK.

They developed acceptance for past coping behaviors and learned to recognize when their ego's harmful story reared its ugly head.

I'm hoping you can begin to see you're not defective for being the way you are or doing the things you've done. It's all been an effort to avoid pain. Who can blame you for that? But we must recognize that the old methods will never bear fruit. To alleviate pain, we must change. If things are to change, we must leave the behind the unhelpful perspective that we are somehow fatally flawed. We must trust we are whole—and know that we have been from the start.

RECOVERING WHO YOU'VE ALWAYS BEEN

Back to moving day. As I double check the house one more time, I find one last box stored in the top of my bedroom closet. I almost forgot it. On my tiptoes, I manage to reach it and set it down on the ground. I chuckle—this is the box of all my old schoolwork my mother couldn't seem to part with. Who knows why I'm still lugging this stuff from move to move, but for some reason, I can't let it go either. I suppose there's something powerful about remembering who we were and revisiting that person from time to time.

Sitting cross-legged on the floor, I rifle through the contents: mostly old finger paintings and spelling tests. Toward the bottom of the box, I find a self-portrait I sketched in preschool, right before the first-grade playground rejection. The drawing depicts a little boy with a bowl haircut, those big Coke-bottle glasses, and a shy smile. I'm wearing a striped shirt. The labored markings spelling my name and the slight smile penciled on my face were drawn by a kid who felt safe in the world. He still knew how to be happy with himself and was wide awake to the life unfolding in front of him. *What did he have that I'm now missing?* I wonder as I place the box in my car and follow the movers to my new place.

A few hours later as I unpack my clothes and arrange my bedroom furniture, I decide to put that self-portrait on the nightstand next to my bed. Every morning, I will see it and think about the person that little boy has become.

What would young Reagan think of me now?

I continue unpacking, now in the living room. I pull books out of boxes and organize them by category on the open shelves. I've spent the last three and a half decades reading every book I can get my hands on about spirituality and personal development, hoping that someday I'll stumble across something—a tool or mindset—I can put into practice to find peace and wholeness again. But for all the books I've read, the TED Talks I've watched, and the reflection I've done about overcoming my fear of inadequacy, I haven't come across a better practice than using our energy to recover who we are instead of trying to discover who we should become.

Bottom line, we get to decide where we direct our efforts. Will we spend our energy holding on to our fears that we are inadequate? Or will we bring awareness to moments our ego tries to overtake us and focus instead on returning to a place of wholeness?

Reagan, as a young sketch artist, already had everything he needed to love and be loved, build relationships, work hard, belong, and create. That's as true today as it was then. Our real work, then, is not to lament about our inability to become who we think we're supposed to be but to find peace in learning to love who we are.

I wish I could invite five-year-old Reagan to my fortieth birthday party. When he showed up, I'd give him a Dr. Pepper and update him on all the new Batman movies. Over the course of the evening, I'd try to share what I've learned in bite-sized pieces he could understand. I'd tell him that it's OK to believe in magic no matter what anyone says, to always be the person who loves deeply, and to keep drawing. I'd tell him it's easy to forget sometimes, but every moment of life can be meaningful. I'd tell him that he belongs even if it doesn't always feel like it.

Toward the end of the evening, for the final impartation, I'd squat down to young Reagan's level and place both my hands on his shoulders. Looking right into his big eyeballs, I'd tell him, "More than anything, I want you to know this: You're OK just the way you are—there's absolutely nothing wrong with you."

And with quiet confidence, I bet he'd whisper, "I know."

I suppose all the hurt, all the emotional reactions, all the years of drinking, and all the time I spent on the sidelines of my life have brought me here—back to the beginning—face to face with a truth that's always been available to me: that I'm OK. Sometimes I still get embarrassed that it's taken me almost thirty years to realize everything got complicated when I started believing my ego's lies about my worth. But it's all right, we need the challenges to wake us up. Our pain is part of our story. None of the time you have spent contending with your own sense of unworthiness is irredeemable.

Our long journey to the brink of self-loathing and back has equipped us to take responsibility for our coping behaviors and have compassion on ourselves for just trying to survive. We can now wake up, see our ego's lies and emotional distractions for what they are, choose to participate in our lives instead of hide, be selfless with others, and believe we're OK. Because, as my sponsor says, we've always been OK.

This will take time. We'll never do it perfectly. We'll learn to love ourselves for simply showing up and giving it a go. I make no promises that you'll ever feel 100 percent confident or secure (does anyone?), but I can give you a road map that's worked for me, my mentors, and the people I've had the privilege of coaching.

Both the hardest and simplest thing we can do now is to start playing the part of a person who no longer believes there's anything wrong with them. We don't even have to believe it yet. But now is the time to move from awareness and acceptance into action.

In the next half of the book, we'll cover concrete steps to help us heal the wounds which have so often kept us isolated.

If you still do not feel understood, I hope you finish this section knowing this: I see you. Never forget, either, that we're not building a case for your defectiveness. We're shining a light on tendencies we've developed as a reaction to difficulties in our lives so we can wake up and make adjustments that will change our relationship with ourselves, others, and our work.

You've done courageous work. Let's press on.

PART TWO

The Growth Path for the Too Emotional

CHAPTER 16

A New Relationship
with Yourself

By this point, I hope you're beginning to see things a little differently. Now is when we start to apply what we've learned. Moving boldly ahead, we're going to explore how you can tap the very awareness you've so diligently created to change your relationship with yourself.

The first half of the book was focused on awareness and organized like this: work, relationships, self. We first uncovered the complications in our work life, then understood how our relationships with others are challenged, and finally saw how our relationship with ourselves is defined and undermined by our sense of inadequacy.

Were we to have started with our internal experience (self) first, our call to growth would have felt less urgent, since we may not have seen all the ways our ego's old stories sabotaged our work and relationships. We had to first take a hard, candid look at the symptoms of our sense of dejectedness before we could truly attend to the deep wound that we feel defective.

Moving into the second half of the book, we're prioritizing action and will proceed in reverse order: self, relationships, and then work. Taking action to heal our relationship with self is the first and most foundational step to showing up in relationships and finding the motivation to persevere and excel in our work. I was reminded of the importance of this when I enrolled in a writer's workshop to help with writing this book.

This workshop's external accountability was just what I needed. Pages are due each week, and you talk through your project with other writers who are also working on their books. But each week, I'm coming up short on my required pages, and when I do produce words, they feel lifeless. I'm beginning to doubt my abilities and worry that I don't have anything of value to offer. After one particular session, I feel especially discouraged, so I let the room clear before approaching the workshop facilitator.

She's got a bob haircut and quick eyes that dart around the room like she's not listening to you. But you get the sense she's not intentionally ignoring you; she's just excited to take everything in.

"I'm not producing anything of value," I tell her, hands jammed in my pockets.

She looks out the window as if the answers are out there, slides her bangs to the side, and asks, "How are you living? How are you treating yourself?"

"How am I . . ." I stutter a response. She interrupts me by repeating the question, then gathers her papers, puts them in a grocery bag, and nods toward the door. I follow her.

We walk around the parking lot like it's a labyrinth, looking at the ground. After a few laps and a long silence, she says, "Good writing comes from good living. If we want to produce something we feel good about, I've found our creative outputs are intimately connected to the quality of our participation in daily life and the kindness we offer ourselves along the way."

She snorts, seeming happy to have articulated her thoughts in the way she did, as if she needed to hear it herself. After a few more paces, we break out of the labyrinth and onto the sidewalk. She can sense from my short breaths that I don't understand. She goes on.

"In the work of writing, or making it through a day, filing insurance claims, or whatever it is you do—you can't wrangle something beautiful out of . . . a husk of a life. If you want to produce something good and true, you gotta learn how to fill up." Seeing that I'm still hungry for a bit more, she admonishes me to "focus less on performance, less on perfection, which are the things we think we need, and more on relaxing and participating—and relaxing means accepting you've got everything you need."

As we approach her car, I tell her about all the times I sit down to write and don't feel like I'm producing anything. I mention that I'm frequently paralyzed by shame and inaction and avoid doing anything at all. She isn't fazed.

"You know what you're gonna get by doing nothing." She smiles. "And you know what the pursuit of perfection will do to you."

I nod.

"It seems to me you've lived most of your life believing top performance will equal satisfactory results, yet you fear you can't perform adequately," she observes. "But I wonder how things might work out differently if you relaxed a bit and didn't expect so much from every single thing you do."

Then, before she drives away, she completes the lesson.

"I suppose you have to decide if you're after a fleeting sense of feeling like you're not a screw-up because you can check all the boxes everyone else checks, or if you're more interested in discovering something meaningful in the midst of your life. Start with you. If you change your objective, you'll be surprised by the results."

I slowly shuffle to my car, sit down, and buckle my seat belt. With both hands on the wheel in the darkness, I think, *Is this all easier than I've been making it out to be?*

PARTICIPATION = DOING THINGS IN REAL LIFE

A few days after the conversation with my writing instructor, I'm with Lily, my white Labrador Retriever, at a spring-fed river, where we're going to spend the afternoon swimming. I've built up this moment so much in my head. This is going to unlock the kind of rich and poetic life I'm looking for.

After this, I'll stop being afraid of the outside world and start participating in my life.

But I'm frozen near the water's edge. This is my first time bringing Lily to the springs, and I don't know what to do next.

This is stupid, I tell myself as I look around at all the people and their dogs jumping in and out of the water. I'm still standing on the trail, baking in the sun, poor Lily beside me panting like an overworked window air conditioning unit.

We're here—we're at the springs—we've done the hard work of showing up, I think. But for some reason, I can't seem to take off my hat and shirt or let Lily off her leash so we can bound together into the fresh water. So what's the hang-up? I'm betting you understand what's happening.

Lily claws my leg impatiently as I look around at the scene. There's a fisherman just a few dozen yards upstream; I don't want to scare away the fish or disrupt his line and piss him off. He probably has a knife in his tackle box.

I see another dog owner let their pup off leash on the opposite bank. She looks at me like I'm doing something wrong. Oh no, did I forget to apply for some sort of dog swimming permit?

I don't want to enter the springs the wrong way. I don't want someone to tell me I'm not supposed to leave my things on that stump or frown at me because dogs aren't welcome on this side of the riverbank.

Our egos can construct countless reasons why we shouldn't participate in our lives and instead entice us to return to the familiar internal emotional drama we've come to depend on. We find ourselves butting up against the one thing standing between us and what we want—and that is the decision to participate.

Participation is scary.

This goes for joining a gym and going to a new workout class. It applies to skiing for the first time and dancing at a honky-tonk.

People like us want all the internal payoff without any of the exposure. But we will not grow, learn, or fully live if we're continuously (and falsely) obsessed with getting things right, looking competent, and ensuring others approve of our particular way of participating. And it is precisely participation in real life that will show us there's nothing wrong with us.

I love the line from Chris McCandless, whose adventurous story was captured in Jon Krakauer's book, *Into the Wild*: "The core of man's spirit comes from new experiences."[1]

Why should we, who care so much about our spirit, exempt ourselves from such a wellspring? Still unconvinced? Teddy Roosevelt's famous words only strengthen the case.

"It is not the critic who counts: not the man who points out how the strong man stumbles or where the doer of deeds could have done better. The credit belongs to the man who is actually in the arena, whose face is marred by dust and sweat and blood, who strives valiantly, who errs and comes up short again and again, because there is no effort without error or shortcoming, but who knows great enthusiasms, the great devotions, who spends himself in a worthy cause; who, at the best, knows, in the end, the triumph of high achievement, and who, at the worst, if he fails, at least he fails while daring greatly, so that his place shall never be with those cold and timid souls who knew neither victory nor defeat."[2]

The power and the paradox of participation is this: For us to get what we really want—to find connection, peace, freedom, joy, and courage—we must dance in real life. We must take action. We must participate. There is no substitute.

Lily and I do eventually find our way into the springs, and it is glorious, like swimming in pure shadows. As I enjoy this new memory with my pup, no one cares about the way we've entered the water. No one is bothered by her splashing and barking and weaving between them as she swims after the tennis ball I lob through the air.

Nothing bad is happening to us. Instead, we're enjoying a moment of deep connection we otherwise would have missed were I to continue obsessing about correctness, perfect performance, and avoiding criticism.

Lily and I drive home like champions with the windows down and our tongues out.

Eventually, new actions and behaviors reshape beliefs. More slowly, our changed beliefs shape how we feel about ourselves. Then, one fine day, we wake up and see we've always been whole and capable. You know by now that this won't happen by thought alone. We must implement practices that show us the truth.

We must set ourselves free through participation.

145

NOTES

1. Jon Krakauer, *Into the Wild* (New York: Villard, 1996).
2. Theodore Roosevelt, "The Man in the Arena" in "Citizenship in a Republic," Sorbonne, Paris, France, April 23, 1910.

CHAPTER 17

Building a Case for Your Worth through Participation

Healing our interior fear of being defective hinges on our willingness to participate in the real world. The antidote to internal sadness is external action.

Problem is, it's not uncommon for people like us to hide from the discomfort of testing new behaviors by thinking self-development is for people who are wired differently.

I get it, I get it. Most personal and professional development material is crafted by highly motivated people, for highly motivated people. When someone like us sets out to implement the habits of the highly successful, we're somehow convinced we'll screw it up before we even try. So we lose faith and abandon the process—which causes us to feel shame and stop participating.

Why can't I just journal about this? our ego cries out. But remember, that's our ego bucking against change. We silence our ego by taking small actions in real life that help us write a new story about ourselves.

We've got to build a case for our worth so we can treat ourselves with more love and compassion. This means putting practices into place that remind us we are our own agents of change. No more waiting for the right emotions to save us.

Here are some practices to shepherd us into participation and support the strengthening of our self-worth.

MORNING SELF-TALK

Remember when I shared how sometimes I'll wake up, snooze my alarm, and immediately fear that I've already screwed up my day? Most folks with a core belief that they're defective report crippling feelings of doubt, shame, envy, and depression before they even get out of bed. This has certainly been the case for me.

We are now aware of our negative self-talk, and we understand we'll blindly believe whatever story our emotions write for us. So we must practice awareness from the moment we open our eyes to begin our days differently.

The following practice was created by BJ Fogg, a social scientist and founder of the Behavior Design Lab at Stanford University. In his book, *Tiny Habits,* he outlines the "Maui Habit" as a way of beginning our days with a different story. The Maui Habit instructs us to simply say to ourselves, when we awaken, "Today is going to be a great day."[1]

That's it. Seems almost too cheesy to work, doesn't it? But think about all the negative things you tell yourself upon waking now, and it's not hard to see why Fogg's research suggests this shift in self-talk could make a real difference.

"By embracing feelings of success and adding more goodness to your day-to-day life, you are making the world brighter not only for yourself, but also for others," Fogg writes in *Tiny Habits*. "You are vanquishing shame and guilt and you are freeing yourself and others who have endured a lifetime of self trash talk."

It's not about creating new practices that ring hollow but changing how you experience your day from your first waking moments.

"The most profound transformations I've shared with you . . . are not about discreet habits being formed," Fogg continues in his book. "They are about essential shifts in experience, from suffering to less suffering, from fear to hope, from being overwhelmed to feeling empowered."

Remember my writing workshop instructor's wisdom: Inputs equal outputs. Behaviors shape beliefs. Thoughts become things. We find what we are looking for. Just try it. What have you got to lose?

I've found it helpful to say the phrase aloud. Sometimes I look in the mirror after brushing my teeth and say some version of "Today is going to be a great day" to help create a different story and direct my emotional energy toward a future I'm excited about.

MEDITATING ON THE FUTURE

People like us claim to be masters of our internal world. But after working with thousands of highly emotional types as an educator, coach, workshop facilitator, and keynote speaker, I've found very few actually practice some sort of prayer or meditation. Some say it's because they don't think they'll do it right. Others report not seeing a difference in their lives, so they give up.

On days I avoid my meditation practice it's normally because I fear that I'm already 30 points behind in the game of life, so I don't have time to waste. I must get started on work because that's the only way I'll get the external affirmation I need.

[Insert your excuse here.]

The power of meditation, like the Maui Habit, has everything to do with shifting our default mental state and changing how we face our day. We must retrain our brains to focus on gratitude, possibility and belonging instead of lack, fear, and shame. The more we practice introducing new thoughts, the more hardwired those new thoughts will become, and the less energy we'll give to negative thoughts that reaffirm our unhelpful feelings.

My morning meditation differs slightly from the common practice of clearing one's mind of all thoughts by focusing on the breath. It involves seeing the future. Though I do spend a few moments breathing and clearing my mind to begin.

The real value of the meditation practice I want you to try involves envisioning your future self encountering the day with excitement, willingness, acceptance, and peace. Find a quiet place, put on some ambient meditation music, and, with your eyes closed, literally see your future self, just moments from now, getting up from the meditation and navigating your day in all the ways you wish you could.

During the meditation, I try to have an actual smile on my face and work to feel gratitude for a well-lived day before the day has even begun.

Drawing on his extensive research on the power of meditation, Dr. Joe Dispenza shares that the emotion of gratitude is the ultimate indicator of having received something, because we generally feel grateful after a positive event has occurred. So if we can practice "pre-gratitude"—feeling grateful for a day well-lived before it has happened—our brain comes to believe those events have already taken place. As a result, we're more likely to get up and act according to the future we envisioned because we're already grateful for it.

This is no different than Michael Jordan visualizing shooting free throws or the mental rehearsal Michael Phelps ran through before each Olympic gold–winning swim. We must train our brains to expect a positive future and feel thankful for its possibility.

At the end of our meditation, when we actually open our eyes and get up, our subconscious goes to work slowly tweaking our lived experience. You'll start to notice you're reacting differently and worrying less. You'll smile more. In my experience, the effects are astonishing and real.

KEEPING A GRATITUDE LIST

An oldie but goodie—put what you're thankful for on paper. Don't even act like you can't do this one. Us emotional types have a journal squirreled away in every room, and it only takes a minute to write down a few things.

Your gratitude can be focused on the past, present, or future. I'm a big fan of being "pre-grateful" and writing down positive things you believe are going to occur ahead of time. The goal is to exercise our positivity muscles and rewire our brains to look for what is going well in our lives. Don't let this devolve into something you *were* grateful for but lost, or the gratitude you *wish* you could have.

Beware of the desire to coopt this practice as a way to journal about your feelings all morning instead of getting on with your day. Write your gratitude list and move on to the next practice.

The purpose of the gratitude list is to prime you to participate, not endorse emotional wallowing.

FAKE IT FOR FIVE

Starting something is often the hardest part, particularly for people like us, since we believe we must *feel* like we're ready to start. We think we must experience all of the emotions we imagine a motivated person feels. If we don't *feel* those emotions, we often never begin. Next thing you know, it's 3:26 in the afternoon and we might as well call it a day.

We'll get into more practices to boost productivity when we turn our attention to work, but this is a building block practice we must start implementing throughout our days. I call it *Fake It for Five*. For some of us, it's going to take a while before we get excited about participating in our daily lives. So in the meantime, we're going to have to fake it—five minutes at a time.

Please, no objections here about valuing authenticity and not wanting to fake anything. I've worn out that record for years, and trust me, when it comes to people like us who are on the fence about participating in our lives, faking it leads to fulfillment.

To execute the *Fake It for Five* maneuver, simply identify an activity you know you need to begin but are less than enthusiastic about starting. It could be work, exercise, cleaning, correspondence, or even the gratitude list above. Now that you've identified the necessary task, set a timer for five minutes.

After you start the timer, your job is to play the part of a person who is motivated to complete the task at hand. Nothing over the top. I don't want you trying to conjure tears of joy as you pay the bills. No one does that. Simply pretend to be the kind of person who tackles a job with ease. Doesn't matter if it's folding laundry or taking a walk.

We're trying to do two things:

1. Get you off your bum by participating.
2. Practice feeling motivated, even if it's pretend.

You can guess what happens. Often after the five minutes is up, you find yourself willing to finish the thing you started. You've got momentum now. You're over the hump. So you might as well keep going.

This works for me every single time I go on a run. Literally, every time. I hate running—that is, until I remind myself how great I feel after exercise. So, I practice the *Fake It for Five* maneuver with 100 percent awareness that I'm attempting to trick myself into liking an activity I loathe. Doesn't matter. I always end up running for longer, and I find myself smiling at the end.

We forget what's good for us. We have to be reminded again every day. Don't feel shame for feeling a lack of motivation. No one wants to battle their ego. No one is doing life perfectly. It's only natural to reject change.

Just pretend you want to participate until you actually do.

CONNECTING WITH OTHERS

People like us cherish our alone time.

We romanticize solitary mornings with coffee and a book. We can idealize walks alone in the woods. We find ourselves drawn to stories of people with large internal worlds.

As a result, we tend to believe we have less energy for human interaction than others. This is not to say we don't enjoy spending time with those we love, but sometimes we can fall prey to the belief that a perfect day is one without interruption from others.

Yet, it's important to remember human contact does us good. One of the best ways to keep from getting lost in our internal world is by engaging with others. The next section on relationships will cover in detail how we can better connect with those in our lives, but I want to include a practice here as we're learning how to more consciously participate in our days.

I tend to view unannounced phone calls and text messages as interruptions. But in the past year I've decided that, unless I'm truly engaged in the momentum of meaningful work, I'll pick up the phone when it rings. I'll respond to a text when it comes through. I'm not doing this out of guilt or shame but to practice getting outside of my internal world and realizing others have something to teach me.

If time is tight, you could answer, "Hey, so good to hear from you. I only have a few minutes, but wanted to pick up and at least say hello."

Again, we're after participation. With others. In real life.

Maybe you have a job where you're required to interact with people all day and you don't need to worry about this one as much. However, if you're like me and a solopreneur, it's easy to string several days together without interaction. Often we *think* we prefer it. So, if I notice my day is wide open, instead of hoarding alone time, I make sure to schedule a coffee or virtual catch-up with someone.

There's nothing wrong with alone time, but sometimes growth only takes place in community. Find ways to make time for people, and, gradually, you'll find you're less obsessed with your own experience, less wary of the motives of others, and more open to ways you can contribute by simply being present with someone else.

FINDING MEANING IN THE MIDST OF YOUR REGULAR LIFE

All of this participation I'm pushing us toward doesn't mean we have to lose track of the best parts of who we are.

We long for depth in all experiences. This can be healthy if we use our desire for meaning to amplify the regular moments of our lives instead of punctuating what's missing. Rather than seeing our days as this collection of mundane practices like positive self-talk, meditation, pretending to like things we don't like, and interacting with others, we can choose to find the magic hidden in our midst.

Once I was hosting a dinner party and ran to the spice rack to grab the salt. The moment I lifted the bottle of white crystals, I saw, through a window, similar whiteness in the dry snowbank in my neighbor's yard, where a light breeze swirled. I thought of my neighbor's son and his lisp and how his life might be hard. I wondered if I might fall for the girl at the table and even one day start a family with her. I smelled the musty basement through an open door, heard the conversation at the dinner table, and all at once felt as if my life had an immense amount of meaning.

That was ten years ago, and every time I pick up a salt-shaker, I still think of that small house in South Dakota where I lived for a few years. When we stop looking for what's missing, we can find meaning in the briefest, seemingly inconsequential moments. We don't have to wait for peak emotional experiences to add substance to our life.

MOVING YOUR BODY AND "CHANGING YOUR BIOLOGY"

I mentioned how *Fake It for Five* has helped me create a healthier relationship with exercise. In working with people like us, I've found exercise is often a sore subject. We feel shame for not being athletic enough, not enjoying working out with other people, or failing to stick to a regimen.

For me, some sort of daily motion serves not only as a way to stay healthy but also as a physical representation of my ability to overcome internal barriers. If I can keep running, do a few more pushups or hold a plank longer than I did yesterday, that confidence can be carried into my battle with antagonizing emotions.

Moving our bodies can change our perspective on reality.

Some days, when I lose sight of what's important, I know I need a hard reset. Whether it's actual exercise or simply getting up from my seat, I take to heart the advice of performance coach Brendon Burchard: "When you're down and out, it's time to get out and about."

Maybe it's deciding to go to the grocery store or take out the trash. Maybe you need to eat something or take a cold shower. Moving our bodies, while staying the course and keeping on task for the day, can make a big difference. Tony Robbins talks about how we're "changing our biology" through these intermittent interventions.[2] In the recovery community, they say, "Move a muscle, change a thought."

We have more energy than we think we do. Laying on the couch under the guise of self-care will not solve our problems. The last thing we want to do when we feel sluggish or tied up in emotional knots is take action or be active, but that's exactly what we need to do. When we participate in life, especially when we don't feel like it, our outlook changes.

TENDING TO YOUR EXTERNAL WORLD

With such rich internal worlds, we often let our external world fall to the wayside. For many years, my apartment was a direct representation of my emotional state: messy. If my feelings were getting the best of me, I'd forget to pay bills, never make my bed, and let dishes pile up in the sink.

I've since learned that when I sense I'm drifting out of reality down my internal elevator, it's time to rack up some small wins in real life. I might pick up the clothes, do the dishes, or mail the wedding RSVP that's been sitting on the counter for a week.

Psychologist Dr. Benjamin Hardy tells us all behaviors are addictive. This can either be good or bad for us. Our ego likes our default behaviors and sees changing them as a loss of self. This is why when we're feeling down we continue to behave as if we're the person who feels down. When our environment is unkept and disorganized, we continue to behave as if that's who we are.

But we've now done the work of realizing we can change. For me, sometimes a reminder of my ability to change comes from low-hanging-fruit activities like tidying up.

"Your behavior doesn't come from your personality," Hardy shares on *The Learning Leader Show* with Ryan Hawk. "Rather, your personality is shaped by your behavior. When you act a certain way, you then judge yourself based on your actions. Hence, you can quickly alter your identity simply by altering your behavior."[3]

When we bring awareness to our emotional behaviors, we can learn to introduce replacement behaviors that allow us to tidy up our lives. This can range from keeping a neat home to getting outside for a walk or run. By staying engaged in our external world, we'll realize emotional benefits we can't access by tending to our inner world alone.

ACCEPTING WHAT COMES

Sometimes, despite all of these strategies, a day just goes sideways.

The participation practices we've covered are highly beneficial, with one caveat: We must not rely on any particular practice to completely fulfill us emotionally. Sometimes a new behavior like exercise or picking up the phone will give us a burst of confidence initially—then the emotional payoff will dwindle over time. If we remain unaware of our ego's desire for emotional stimulation, we can sometimes lose faith in new practices when they either stop feeling as powerful as they once did or fail to work in a certain situation.

It's essential for us to remember we'll never have total control over our external circumstances, no matter how much we might fantasize that this new practice will allow "the new us" to live a life free of pain. Bad days still happen. We'll get down on ourselves. People will disappoint us. Work will present us with new challenges.

We will lose steam when putting our faith in new behaviors *alone*. We may see a bad day as evidence that we just couldn't do the behaviors correctly. Then down the internal elevator we go again. This is the real moment of truth for us. Instead of engaging in old stories about our defectiveness, we must accept reality for what it is and look for another way to participate.

In fact, hard as it may be to embrace what we can't anticipate, we should welcome the unexpected. Real disappointments and unpredictable events offer us an opportunity to see that we have everything it takes to participate in this life even when we're caught unawares. Author and coach Chris McAlister says it's rare we have a perfect day, but if we practice accepting what unfolds in front of us, we can create beautiful weeks.

CELEBRATING OURSELVES

I don't know about you, but I have a hard time celebrating myself. This makes sense when one is unconscious to their default belief that they're nothing special.

The past few years when Elle held a birthday party for me, she insisted we take a moment to go around the room so each person can share something they love about me. It's uncomfortable, and I can barely stand the silence between shares. But, year after year, I'm learning to relax and, with gratitude, realize I am worthy of being celebrated. Not for being the best at something or more special than anyone else, but simply for being a person who has navigated another year as best he could.

My friend Murray is one of us. He's an artist's artist. He recently told me how, before he sits down to tackle a complex design project, he often holds a private dance party for himself in his office. He lights some incense and celebrates his willingness to do the work by dancing alone to Outkast.

For many of us, life can seem so heavy and the work before us so daunting that we scarcely consider we've finished anything worthwhile or accomplished anything of note. But if we fail to recognize our forward motion, we'll never be able to stick to any of the practices listed here. Even if you only accomplish healthier morning self-talk, complete a gratitude list, or take your dog on a walk, recognize *you* inspired yourself to participate in your life. And that is an improvement on the days when you would have otherwise retreated into your internal world of emotions.

In his book *The Gap and The Gain: The High Achievers' Guide to Happiness, Confidence, and Success*, author and coach Dan Sullivan shares how we'll never move out of the trap of comparison and shame if we focus on the gap between where we are and where we think we should be. Instead, we must focus on how far we've come.[4] Even if we only gained an inch, that's forward progress.

Choosing to implement any of the practices we've covered means you've finished something you started, you've chosen to be a little better than you were yesterday, and you can do it all again tomorrow. That, my friend, is worth a small celebration if not a private dance party. Make time at the end of each day to recognize what you did to pull yourself out of your emotions and push yourself into the world.

Consider and heed author and habits expert James Clear's encouragement:

"Finish something. Anything. Stop researching, planning and preparing to do the work and just do the work. It doesn't matter how good or how bad it is. You don't need to set the world on fire with your first try. You just need to prove to yourself that you have what it takes to produce something. There are no artists, athletes, entrepreneurs or scientists who became great by half-finishing their work. Stop debating what you should make and just make something."[5]

I hope these practices seem possible, and I pray that you believe you have the ability to put a few of them to work on your journey to remind yourself, through participation, that you are capable, worthy, and equipped.

It's worth reiterating that the goal is not to sever our connection with our emotions or extinguish our internal world by forcing ourselves to do a bunch of things we don't want to do. Our connection to our emotions will never leave us.

We're simply learning to turn down the volume on our internal world as we are now aware of how our egos have kept us from participating in real life by distracting us with shame.

Start small with the practices above. Consistency is key. Over time, you're going to witness yourself unconsciously choosing to clean up the house, answering the phone with confidence, going on a run when overwhelmed by emotions, or talking to yourself with more compassion. You'll begin to see beauty everywhere and find meaning anywhere as you come to believe it is your unfolding life—not your internal sense of inadequacy—that is the story you were meant to experience.

These little actions add up, and a greater sense of self-worth is the reward.

Next, we'll explore how we can enrich our interactions with others by learning strategies to participate in our relationships from a place of selflessness.

NOTES

1. BJ Fogg, *Tiny Habits* (Harvest, 2020).
2. Tony Robbins, "What Is Biohacking? Everything You Need to Know about Biohacking Your Body," *Tony Robbins*, https://www .tonyrobbins.com/health-vitality/biohacking-for-beginners.
3. Benjamin Hardy in "Episode #448: Dr. Benjamin Hardy—How to Go from the Gap to the Gain, Choosing Your Who, & Setting Big Goals," *The Learning Leader Show*, November 28, 2021, https:// learningleader.com/drbenjaminhardy.
4. Dan Sullivan, *The Gap and The Gain: The High Achiever's Guide to Happiness, Confidence, and Success* (Hay House Business, 2021).
5. James Clear, "3-2-1: Craving the result versus the process, seeing clearly, and thinking for yourself," *James Clear*, February 9, 2023, https://jamesclear.com/3-2-1/february-9-2023.

CHAPTER 18

A New Relationship with Others

Rhonda is my favorite barista even though Rhonda is not the best barista.

With spiky gray hair and sharp wit, she's less interested in the business of coffee and more interested in the people buying the coffee. During early-morning rushes, Rhonda holds up the line to talk with every single person about what's going on in their world.

Her approach to selling coffee reminds me of when I waited in line for three hours to get a book signed by the humorist David Sedaris. When I finally arrive in the room where he's stationed, frustrated to be sure, it becomes clear why things are taking so long. He asks questions of each person whose book he signs, inviting them to tell a story about who they are. As they share their story, he patiently draws something in their book and signs his name. Each of us walks away with a strange drawing and a sense of importance.

Rhonda the barista honors people in her own way by asking about trips they've recently taken. Over time, I notice a pattern. When she learns a patron is going away on an adventure, she hollers out over the hissing steam wands: "Have fun, honey, and bring me back a rock!"

I wonder if any of Rhonda's regulars have ever actually done this. Has any customer returned from a trip to order a latte and, when tendering payment, carefully slid a smooth river stone or pebble from a beach they visited across the counter?

When I ask Rhonda about her life, she says, "Psh—same ole stuff. Tell me about you, baby!"

She's more interested in other people. It's so beautiful I can barely handle it some mornings.

In that same coffee shop, I often sit a few tables over from Zeke, an older gentleman in a flat cap who gets dropped off by a bus early in the morning and stays past the time I leave. With him are his drawing utensils. He labors to set up his art station, but he rarely draws anything because he's consumed with helping Rhonda keep the place clean. When a guest leaves a napkin or fails to properly bus their table, he leaps to bring order to the area.

One morning, Rhonda asks me to bring her back a rock from my upcoming trip to New Mexico. I say I will then claim a table next to Zeke to do some writing. Zeke is pretending to draw, but he's actually more interested in me. I do my best to focus on writing as he stares at the side of my face. Finally, he scoots his chair in my direction, elbows me, and hands over a fifty-cent piece.

I take it cautiously. After staring at Kennedy's engraving for a moment, I shift my gaze from the coin to the window. The darkness of the early morning keeps me from seeing what's outside. Instead, I see our reflection in the glass—my hair parted like JFK's and Zeke looking at me, looking at us.

How much longer will this old man have a reflection? I wonder.

"1971 was a good year—you'll want to hang onto this," he tells me. Then he jumps up and nearly loses his cap as he rushes to tend to a spill on the other side of the restaurant.

"Rhonda and Zeke seem to be more interested in everyone in this place than they are with themselves," I write in my journal that morning. "What would it look like for me to do the same? What if my life is not all about me?"

As I close my journal, pocket the half-dollar, and pack my things, I remember my old college mentor, Earl.

Once a week, I'd wander into his office and lament about not having close relationships with others and not knowing what I wanted to do with my life. He'd swivel in his chair and listen. He never adopted an air of judgment or cut me off. When I finished, he'd pause for a moment as if he was going to say something different than what he said last week. After a long silence, he'd stop swiveling the chair, lock eyes, and say kindly (again): "Reagan—you're forgetting—it's not about you. When will you stop playing the victim and get out there and help somebody?"

End of lesson.

Earl passed away over ten years ago, and I wish like hell he was still around to guide me. At his funeral, they couldn't fit all the people inside the church. The crowd literally spilled out the front door, down the stairs, and onto the sidewalk.

He died a wealthy man—in full possession of the things we're all after: a sense of belonging, a purpose that served people, and a full heart.

He showed me and countless others how, at the end of our lives, those few intangible elements are what the whole game is all about. In every conversation, he reminded me that none of the accomplishments I craved would come to pass if I kept the focus trained on myself and ignored the needs of others.

Over the years as I've endeavored to implement his guidance, I often think in frustration, *How am I going to get anything done if I'm concerned about everyone else? I'm trying to create a business to help other people, for crying out loud. Can't I focus on my needs and my direction for a minute?*

I'm learning to see that Earl never advised me to sacrifice my desires and hopes for the sake of others. He never encouraged me to let distractions and requests from people invade every minute of my day. What he wanted me to remember is that the greatest stories ever told are about a character who wants something for themselves, yes, but also (and more importantly) finds a way to use their life to benefit others. In doing so, they find what we're all after anyway: a sense of belonging, a purpose that serves others, and a full heart.

When we learn to look at our lives and careers as a springboard for helping others, we put into practice the timeless wisdom of that famous salesman and motivational speaker, Zig Ziglar: "You can get everything in life you want if you will just help enough other people get what they want."[1]

Making our lives about others is a generative cycle that's almost too good to be true. When we pull our energy out of our internal experience and direct it toward meeting the needs of people around us, we are actually healing our wounds of defectiveness. It is through our willingness to understand and validate the experiences of others that we discover we're not so different from everyone else. We see everyone has needs, everyone feels pressure, everyone hurts. We're not the only ones with problems. We're not so broken after all.

We get this gift of equanimity when we challenge our ego's impulse to make interactions about us, fight for attention, or assume others are conspiring against us. We find the belonging we've been yearning for when we give like we've got nothing to lose.

NOTE

1.   Zig Ziglar, *Secrets of Closing the Sale* (Revell, 1984).

CHAPTER 19

It's Not about You

Already feeling—based on the chapter title, per-haps—like this is going to be a tough pill to swallow? Think of the call to action here not so much as an admonishment but as a reframing. Remembering that our lives are not about us has everything to do with adopting new perspectives.

For example, do you still believe all your energy is best spent reconciling your emotions and fighting for affirmation? Or, while validation is important, are you able to see the bigger picture? Can you see how our communities and lives collectively get better when we take small actions every day that move us closer to one another?

It's up to each of us to manage our emotional life. That's no one else's job, and we'll miss out on the joy of relationships if we put pressure on others to make us feel OK. By default, people like us can be incredibly self-referencing.

When we're unaware of our emotions, we scarcely have the energy to tend to relationships with others.

But as Rhonda, Zeke, and Earl show us, making life about others ensures we ultimately get what we really want, and that is connection. We both heal our pain and improve our relationships when we provide those in our lives with the sense of belonging we so desperately desire.

Here are a few perspectives we must internalize to strengthen relationships. They will help us make interactions with others about their experiences, needs, and wants—not just ours.

REALIZE THAT FEW PEOPLE CAN STOMACH ALL YOUR EMOTIONS

I'm sitting in my therapist's office sharing my feelings about a recent interaction with a friend. This friend has let me down again. My feelings of disappointment toward him and our relationship are hard to shake.

"I think we need to have another conversation about our friendship," I say to my therapist, looking at her with determination.

She seems to choke on her tongue, then nearly jumps out of her seat. "Whoa, Nellie! Maybe not," she exclaims. "You've already had a few conversations about how you're feeling toward him."

My therapist cautiously sits back in her chair and tries to relax. She hits her asthma inhaler a couple times. She then says with all the kindness she can manage, "Reagan, you have to remember not everyone swims in the deep waters of emotions like you. Look, I don't want you to hear this the wrong way, but you're going to wear people down if you insist on making sure your each and every emotion is communicated and processed."

This is hard to receive. Especially for people like us who already believe we're burdensome, defective, or overbearing. But it's true. I'm friends with people like you and me. I've been on the receiving end of a relationship where the other person believes we have to pick apart each thing they're feeling all the time. It's exhausting, and it makes me want to engage less in the relationship.

Of course, that doesn't mean I don't care for these friends. But I can tell you I'm often less than excited when I anticipate being around them because I know it's going to drain my energy. I have to psych myself up and remember I'm about to get nothing out of this particular interaction and they're going to expect everything.

Sounds exhausting, right? With gentleness, I ask you to bring awareness to times you've put others in a similar situation.

Take a breath before putting the weight of your feelings on someone else. Create some space before coloring their reality with every emotion you're experiencing. Remember, you're trying to find freedom from your emotions, not overwhelm others.

I like to apply what we'll call the 20/80 rule to sharing feelings: Only talk about what you're feeling 20 percent of the time. Out of five hangouts with a friend, only hit them with your emotions one time. During a workweek, pick one day to have a conversation with a coworker about what you're experiencing emotionally. No more.

No need to feel shame about this. We know better than that. This isn't about you. This is about realizing others aren't wired the same as us while we simultaneously work to mature and be considerate of their time and energy. Let's give others a reason to be excited to see us and not hit them with the deep cuts in every interaction.

RECOGNIZE THAT OTHERS WILL NEVER FULLY MEET YOUR NEEDS

I'm in the fifth grade, and my mom just dropped me off at school after an eye doctor appointment. You'll recall that ever since the first grade, I've been the dork with glasses that make my eyes look cartoonishly big—until today. I just got contacts, and everything is about to change.

I return to school during lunch hour to make my debut, fresh from the optometrist's. Besides dispensing with the Coke-bottle glasses, I've changed into a Chicago Bulls sweatshirt, put on an arrowhead necklace, and donned sunglasses I purchased at Six Flags over the summer in preparation for this moment.

I've also got McDonald's for lunch.

I enter the cafeteria and walk across the room just like I planned and sit down at my class-assigned table next to NeTassha. I look to the left, then to the right.

"'Sup," I say.

NeTassha looks at me for a while, trying to figure out what's different. She takes a sip of her chocolate milk without breaking eye contact, then turns around and continues talking to her friends. I look around at everyone, waiting for it to hit them—but it never happens.

Eventually Steven pipes up, "Hey, Reagan."

I turn to him with my whole face, now unobstructed by the heavy machinery of my Donald Duck glasses, and say, "'Sup?"

He looks at me for a long moment and says, "Can I have a french fry?"

Most resentments I have toward others are rooted in my frustration that they don't always meet my needs. Wouldn't it be great if our relationships gave us all the things we wanted all the time? Sure, but it will never happen.

After the totally disappointing premiere of "Reagan with Contacts," I rationalize the whole debacle by thinking, *Of course I didn't get what I wanted. I didn't clearly let others know what I needed.*

This is an easy fix! All I have to do is explicitly outline my needs to others. Then I won't have to encounter the pain and disappointment of feeling unnoticed again. So, for the next twenty-five years, I decide to be the guy who makes his expectations and boundaries in relationships *painfully* clear. Along the way, I amass exponentially more resentments and become angrier than ever at others for continuing to not meet my needs. Because now they aren't failing to meet my needs out of ignorance. Now they're choosing not to give me what I need after I've clearly expressed what I require.

Elle insists upon leaving a trail of her belongings around the house like she has a hole in her purse. Lipstick, phone, credit card, phone charger, laptop charger, crumpled up receipt, stupid koozie from a wedding two years ago—you name it. She does this even though I've repeatedly made it clear that I need order in our home.

No matter how many times I ask my mother to not over-parent me, she will always ask, "Did you say hello to all your cousins?" Every single Christmas. Without fail.

How can this be? Why can I not control others by telling them how I want them to behave? Logically, you'd think if I give someone instructions for being in a relationship with me, then it would be simple to adhere to the rules. Yet time and time again, I find myself disappointed.

At some point, if we're actually interested in beating back our egos and evolving into our higher selves, we must ask if it's other people's fault for not giving us what we need? Or is it our bad for expecting everyone else to dutifully play by *our* rules?

When we zoom out and think about this objectively, hopefully we can see how foolish it is to expect every person in our lives to meet our excessive relational demands. Think of the myriad of things they have to think about each day. Yet somehow we still expect they'll have the additional capacity to make sure we always get the affirmation, respect, and attention we crave. What if we stopped holding people to such high standards?

What if we remembered that, for people like you and me, relationships work best when we stop making everything about us and our needs? Instead of fighting to get our needs met all the time, what if we brought awareness to what we want from others and learned to give it to ourselves?

When we get serious about our own growth and freedom, we see how our disappointment in others for not meeting our needs is just another way to avoid being self-sufficient. If we can continue blaming others, we don't have to bring awareness to our ego's lies and take action to change course.

But we want a new life.

We want freedom.

So we must set others free of our expectation that they meet our emotional needs. Along the way, we'll realize we too have been set free.

UNDERSTAND, NO ONE IS OUT TO GET YOU

Elle and I adopted our dog, Lily. She had a whole life before us. Sadly, she came with some anxiety, which is often the case for rescue dogs. It took Lily years to feel comfortable doing little things like jumping in our bed and snuggling because whatever happened before had conditioned Lily to be cautious and scared.

We're not much different.

We all bear emotional wounds, whether inflicted by others or the story we tell ourselves (normally both), and as a result, we carry with us a wariness when interacting with others. Our brain's outdated programming is wired to keep us safe—which often manifests as a false belief that others aren't safe or that relationships will always end up hurting us. Whether we think people are purposely withholding connection, criticizing with the intent to harm, or silently judging us, we can waste valuable energy believing we must always be on guard.

Yet we now know most of our beliefs about how others intentionally try make us feel unworthy are rooted in our core belief that we are unworthy. We believed it first. The truth is, most things aren't personal. But our penchant for making everything personal can strain relationships when someone's behavior pricks our ego.

Anytime Elle shares a way in which I've hurt her, my default response is, "So I must be a terrible person, huh? Can you not see all of the good things I do for you? You're just going to spend all of your time looking for ways I let you down?" If I give in to the insecurities of my ego, I miss the moment for connection. I fail to rise to the occasion by giving Elle what I also hope to receive in our relationship: the gift of being seen, heard, and respected for how I feel.

As for our fear that others have a litany of negative opinions about us that they keep to themselves or share behind our backs—we just have to let that go. We can only control our decision to practice awareness and acceptance, then take right action. If someone does have an issue with us, it's almost certainly far less extreme than the awful things we're imagining.

I tell myself the following (which comes from my wise friend Andrae) when I'm anxious about others' unexpressed negative opinions of me: "If someone has a problem with me, and they haven't told me they have a problem with me, I choose to believe we don't have a problem."

FREE OTHERS FROM YOUR MOODINESS

Recently, my friend Bart had to tell me he wasn't going to come through on a commitment he made. We're driving home after having dinner, and he slowly wades into the conversation.

"Hey man, I know I told you I'd be able to meet you guys earlier in the day for your bachelor party," he says, "but some work stuff came up, so I'm going to have to just show up for dinner."

I can sense his nervousness.

The poor guy is doing his best to love me because I've conditioned him to fear letting me down. I've punished him in the past when he's been late or double-booked himself when we were supposed to hang out. Old me would have been proud that I finally managed to scare people in my life enough to think twice before not meeting my expressed needs. But friendships aren't about rules, are they? They're about doing life together.

I look at Bart with newfound compassion for both of us. "No sweat, man. It means so much you'll be there at all."

I can now see with clarity the instances in my life when I've conditioned people I love to walk on eggshells for fear of upsetting me. When I'm home for Christmas with my family, everyone is super cautious to make sure Reagan doesn't get in a mood. Elle worries about bringing things up that once sent me into an emotional tailspin. Friends are afraid to invite me to do things last minute because I once made it abundantly clear I wanted them to respect my time by planning things with me in advance.

What a waste of energy.

I invite you to bring awareness to times in your relationships when you've worked to force people into treating you a certain way because you believe their compliance equals love. Real love for others means we accept them for who they are. In most cases, it's best to let the small things slide and focus on the thing we really desire: connection.

COMMUNICATE YOUR NEEDS IN A DIFFERENT WAY

I hope the lessons thus far haven't caused you to believe your needs don't matter. That's not true. If you're in an unhealthy relationship with a person who clearly doesn't value you, that might be a relationship you should exit. I'm trusting you can honestly assess the difference between a person who is objectively not good for you and someone who might just miss the mark every once in a while.

Though our growth is all about focusing less on our needs, there are certainly times when we should speak up for ourselves. Our work here is learning how to have a conversation that plainly communicates how we feel without blaming or shaming people in our lives.

I love the vulnerability that researcher, author, and speaker Brené Brown recommends practicing when wading into an uncomfortable conversation about our emotional needs. She says to start the sentence with this phrase: "The story I'm telling myself is . . ."

This simple sentence starter allows us to frame the conversation around our current and limited perspective, which we willingly admit might not be the full picture.

- "After you made that joke about me the other night, I started telling myself a story that you think I'm unorganized and undisciplined. Can you help me set the record straight?"
- "I'm telling myself a story that you don't value one-on-one hangouts anymore because every time we plan something you invite other people . . . I just want to know I'm still an important person to you."
- "When you give me critical feedback on my creative work, I start to tell myself a story that my contributions always come up short. To be clear, that's my story. I want to both give you what you're looking for and feel like I can deliver work that feels authentic to me. Can we talk this through?"

It's best not to use this technique when you're emotionally reactive. If your feelings are hurt, it's a good idea to wait until the next interaction after you've had the chance to cool down. In a day or two, if your higher self believes a conversation is still helpful, ask that person if you can talk through something with them.

When we own the perspective we're bringing into a conversation instead of placing blame on the other party, and when we invite them to help us rewrite the story we're telling ourselves, we can create healthy interactions without an emotional charge.

ACCEPT APOLOGIES THE FIRST TIME

Not long ago, Elle was prescribed a new face wash by her dermatologist that contains peroxide. A few days later, I notice the gray bath towel she's using is turning orange; it's being bleached by the peroxide.

I do my best to calmly bring this to her attention. I let her know those bath towels were given to me by my mother when she helped me move into my new apartment after I quit my corporate job, downsized, and started building my own business. The towels were a gift representing the love of my mother and a new beginning for me. (I know, I know—people like us can romanticize anything.)

I ask Elle to please be careful and only use that towel from now on since it's already been bleached. The next day, I hop out of the shower ready to start my day and notice my gray bath towel is also turning orange. I'm becoming increasingly frustrated as I bring this to Elle's attention. She apologizes profusely for her mistake and really feels bad.

The next day she turns a *third* towel orange.

Three towels.

"I screwed up—big time," she sighs. "You asked me several times to pay more attention and I didn't. I'm so sorry."

But I still won't let it go, and I take digs at her despite her sincere apologies. I manage to make her suffer for days afterward. *Over towels.*

We don't need to keep people in a negative experience because we're the ones who choose to remain there. This doesn't mean we allow others to walk all over us, but when they own a mistake, sincerely apologize, and do their best to rectify the situation, we must accept that's all they can do.

The rest is up to us.

RECOGNIZE THAT OTHERS' NEEDS ARE DIFFERENT FROM YOURS

I'm having coffee with an old colleague to catch up about her new job. She's really enjoying the role, but during our conversation, she mentions a few challenges and shares a couple of her insecurities.

Immediately, I latch onto the insecurities and decide to run with that theme because I've got lots of experience in that department. I ask her to tell me more about her impostor syndrome and how it affects her life. I invite her to dig into her anxiety around what others think and relish in the mistakes she tells me she's made so far. A half-hour into the conversation, she stops, sits up in her chair, and says, "I don't like where this is going. Can we switch gears?"

I look at her quizzically. "What do you mean?"

She holds her coffee mug with both hands and draws it close to her chest. "I really like this job, Reagan," she says, "and I feel like all we're doing is picking apart everything that's wrong with it."

Sometimes we're so desperate for proof that we aren't the only ones who experience difficulty in our lives that we can overly identify with the pain of others and set up base camp there. Not everyone has the same needs as us. Yes, we have a gift for intuiting emotions and being a safe person for others to explore their feelings with, but we must only go there when invited.

Most of the time, the best way to love someone is to let them drive the emotional direction of the conversation. Often just showing up to listen is enough. You don't always have to swim in the deep end and uncover difficult emotions to connect meaningfully with others.

Sometimes small talk is an act of service.

LET OTHERS FEEL WHAT THEY NEED TO FEEL

We want permission to feel the way we feel. So why do we sometimes lose patience with others when they experience emotional turbulence? This can happen, for example, when we're riding high but someone else is having a low day. We don't like it when we finally feel happy but others don't match our energy.

I have an old coworker who is relentlessly happy. I mean you can put your money on him being in a good mood. On a work trip, we find ourselves with free time in Chicago. I'm feeling good about myself and the work we're doing. As we wrap up for the day, I'm ready to go out.

He sighs and looks around the hotel lobby. He shuts his laptop and leans his head back, closing his eyes. "I'm not so sure I'm up to it," he says.

"Come on . . ." I urge him.

He points his head toward me and opens his eyes. "No, dude. I'm in a funk. I need some time to myself." It's not unlike me at the dance hall where you and I first met.

But I don't care about his feelings and proceed to guilt trip him for not being adventurous. I get him to go with me to a bar, and we have an awful time, for which I blame him. In the Uber back to the hotel, he chuckles and says to me, "It's funny how you get a wild hair once in a blue moon. Otherwise you're the one who's moody. But every time Reagan's in a good mood and ready to have some fun, everyone else needs to get on board."

The first thing I should have remembered is that no external circumstance, including my buddy being on a different emotional frequency, needs to influence the way I choose to feel.

Secondly, it would have been nice of me to remember to give my buddy what I want from him: freedom and permission to navigate emotions without feeling guilt or shame.

We must learn to let someone's emotional experience be theirs. We need to be careful not to overidentify with others' suffering or expect them to be up for anything when we're feeling great. Let others be however they need to be. It's not about us.

Lastly, avoid trying to change someone else's emotional state. We wouldn't want others to try to "fix" us, so we shouldn't attempt to do the same. Let us not fall into the trap of shirking our own work by either rejecting or taking ownership of the emotional state of others.

TRUST THAT YOU DON'T HAVE TO PERFORM

How often do you find yourself wanting to bail on all your social commitments?

Is it because you feel like you have to be "on" in group settings?

Back in the day when Elle and I were getting ready to go to a party or dinner with friends, I'd spend an hour complaining about how anxious I felt. "Can't we just cancel?" I'd plead. After doing this work, it's become clear that my lack of interest in social engagements is rooted in my fear that I'm going to have to bring a ton of energy, offer a super-unique perspective, or guide conversations to deep and meaningful places. All so I can live up to the expectations I imagine everyone has of me.

But we now know that no one is thinking about you and me. At all. They're just going to a party to have a good time. Nothing is expected of us. What if we learned to relax and believe that showing up to a party is all we need to do?

This reminds me of my days in improv theater. Every show, I felt immense pressure to perform in every scene. The lights would go off at the end of a scene, and when they came back on, whoever felt like taking the stage was invited to do so. Sometimes people in my troupe would sit out three of six scenes. Not me. I always felt like I had to show up and make my unique contribution. I found myself taking the stage for every single scene, not out of confidence but because I wanted to prove my worth.

One evening after a show, my improv instructor pulls me aside and says, "Reagan, I love the enthusiasm—way to hustle for stage time. But I've got a challenge for you: sit a few out next time. Let the rest of the troupe do some work and see how you can support the scenes they develop."

Human interaction isn't about performing or impressing. It's simply about the connection people can create when they show up with curiosity and openness.

BELIEVE YOU HAVE A GIFT TO GIVE

Most of the perspective shifts we've covered are, of course, meant to illustrate our blind spots. We've all got room for growth. But I also want to highlight the big gift we bring to our relationships.

We have a deep familiarity with all the feelings on the emotional spectrum, while many others only readily experience a few. We're introspective, reflective, and honest about the hard parts of life. We're not easily scared when someone expresses negative feelings about themselves or their circumstances.

We can speak the language of pain, isolation, and self-doubt. And now, because we've learned how to selflessly show up in relationships, we can show others the way out. We can help them see that their feelings don't make them defective. We can let them know they belong even if they don't feel like they do.

We can also speak the language of poetry, beauty, and awe. When we're conscious, we can bring meaning to the mundane parts of life. Please don't miss the ways your journey has made you both emotionally strong and available; you can now support others as both a witness and a guide when their emotions seem too big to handle.

I love what pediatrician, bestselling author, and professor of integrative medicine Dr. Rachel Naomi Remen says about the power of using our experience to serve others:

"Wounding and healing are not opposites. They're part of the same thing. It is our wounds that enable us to be compassionate with the wounds of others. It is our limitations that make us kind to the limitations of other people. It is our loneliness that helps us to find other people or to even know they're alone with an illness. I think I have served people perfectly with parts of myself I used to be ashamed of."[1]

It is our very wounds that now make way for healing.

Because so much of our lives is centered around our heart's experience, relationships can prove very challenging for us. Every instinct we have rises up in protest when we feel like we're overlooked or unattended to by others. I'm hoping you're now able to see with more clarity that our relationships are not threatened by our unlovability but by our fear that we are unlovable.

When we can internalize that everyone wants to belong and be seen for who they are, we can consciously choose to make the first move and give our attention to others.

Now let's take our newfound desire to participate and our willingness to enrich our relationships by taking the focus off ourselves and explore how this helps us find the freedom, confidence, and motivation to make meaningful contributions in our work.

You are growing in ways you can't even see yet.

NOTE

1.   Commonly attributed to Rachel Naomi Remen.

CHAPTER 20

A New Relationship with Work

I'm sitting in a coffee shop wearing whatever I want, completely in control of my time and being paid well to be the chief storyteller at a global consulting firm. In this role, I get to craft ways to tell the stories of the work we do with our clients. It's pretty cool. Yet I'm spinning the same sad song about not feeling connected to what I do. I'm frustrated by the mundane parts of the work, wishing I felt more inspired.

To make it worse, I've just been given a new responsibility to run the firm's newsletter, and I'm stewing. I'm hotter than my coffee because I've just been reminded by my boss, Laura, that she prefers the newsletter goes out early Friday mornings. It's 10 a.m. on Friday, I've yet to publish, and I've got no intention of making it happen before lunch.

What is my deal?

If I were watching a film about me in my twenties, I'd want to slap my ungrateful, self-obsessed, narcissistic face.

Today, if I had an employee who wasted time and resources the way I did then, I'd send them packing. I'm disappointed by how long it took me to wake up to the reality that we all have to work. We must all experience what it's like to be beginners and do things we don't want to do—not only to make an income but also to remind our egos we're no more or less important than anyone else.

I'm sure there have been days when your work fails to fulfill your desires for affirmation and validation. I wonder if you, like me, think you should have all the responsibility without any of the experience? Have you ever wanted all the praise without any of the effort?

Maybe, as I did, you've read seemingly every personal and professional development book about finding your passion but still can't seem to find yours. This makes you envious of those who appear to invest themselves in their work with little effort and find fulfillment along the way. Perhaps you also resent anyone who reminds you of your lack of professional progress. So you wind up unhappy with yourself, disappointed in your work, and pissy with everyone who expects something of you or doesn't think you're special.

As we are waking up, the truth we must come to realize is work is not the enemy. People who expect things from us in exchange for money are not evil. Spending time in the pursuit of professional progress is not an abandonment of our authenticity.

What's more, we are no more or less capable than anyone else when it comes to showing up, making a contribution, and following through. I've learned the secret for people like you and me. It's quite simple. We must learn to get better at making boring, regular, unsexy contributions.

Let's go back to the coffee shop where I'm avoiding sending out that newsletter on a Friday morning.

Gross, I think as I look through the content I'm supposed to share in the weekly publication: birthdays, baby announcements, new team member profiles, photos of staff at different client sites, and updates about health insurance and retirement accounts. In order to gather all of these dumb things, I have to spend precious time every week pestering everyone in the firm to submit poorly lit pictures of their team dinner at Applebee's. This is neither enjoyable nor fulfilling. It feels like it's a waste of my time and talent. I don't like being told what to do or how to do it, and I certainly don't like being forced to do things I deem meaningless.

But I've got to send this newsletter out, and I'm already hours late. I call my dad, who patiently listens to me complain, though I can only imagine how tired he is of my grumbling. He offers encouragement and challenges me to think about ways I might make a meaningful contribution as I approach this mundane task.

"There's probably a way for you to sprinkle in a little *Reagan* here," he says. "See if you can make it fun."

He tells me he loves me and that he's proud of me and we get off the phone. It's now almost lunchtime, and the newsletter is still unfinished.

I get a refill on coffee and return to my laptop, wasting more time by rereading a draft of a blog post I wrote earlier in the morning. I'm in the habit of posting to my personal blog every week or so, and I block time every day to write creatively. I'd rather review my self-proclaimed profound thoughts than do the work I'm paid to do.

The newsletter this week is light because I failed to spend the time asking anyone at the firm for their baby pictures. I need to come up with some content—stat. As I reread the personal blog I'm crafting, I come upon a nice little piece about finding beauty in small moments.

There could be something here, I think.

I spend a few minutes repurposing the content into an introduction to the newsletter and create a "Letter from the Editor" section. I close my eyes, hit send, and go on with my day.

Sometime Saturday afternoon, I check my email and find a few messages from people at the firm thanking me for the reminder to enjoy each moment. The following week, I write another "Letter from the Editor" to begin the newsletter with an anecdote about the power of relationships. Someone writes back almost immediately to thank me for the reminder; they say it had been a hard week and they needed a shot of encouragement.

Slowly, writing the weekly newsletter becomes the most important part of my work. I begin to think all week about ways to bring more purpose and meaning to the firm. This assignment I had detested evolves into a way for me to make a truly unique, meaningful, and incredibly fulfilling contribution.

To this day, when I see old coworkers, they still mention how they miss those weekly insights. In fact, it was the newsletter I never wanted to write that shaped the tone and direction of this book. An opportunity to make meaningful contributions at a high level was hidden in plain sight.

If you're the kind of person who believes your work could and should be fulfilling, you have to realize one thing above all else: Your ability to engage in fulfilling work is entirely up to you.

What do you wish others called on you for? Look for ways to make a contribution more aligned with what you want to do and who you want to be, then start running mini experiments. If you've got to deliver a data-heavy weekly report, for example, could you include a story or testimonial to make it more human? If you're responsible for running a regular meeting that's feeling stale, can you find a way to create connection, belonging, and (gasp) fun at the beginning and end of the gathering? Could you imagine a more creative way to do client follow-ups? Maybe you could start a book club at work or a weekly off-site lunch or invite coworkers to join you on a walk outside on a beautiful day. What is meaningful to you? Try it! Rarely have I heard a boss or manager squash an employee's desire to bring more meaning and connection to the team.

Your direction won't be completely clear in the beginning, and some of your experiments will fail. You'll try to add value to a project and hear crickets. You'll think you've found a fulfilling way to approach a responsibility, but it loses its luster and you have to pivot. That's OK.

The most inspiring career trajectories often involve someone who decides to make something new out of what they've been handed. They wake up one day and realize no employer, supervisor, or market is ever going to bend over backward to provide them with the perfect circumstances or opportunities they think they need. We must get hip to the idea that others aren't spending their time developing solutions for us to make our lives and careers more fulfilling.

Author, speaker, and podcaster Rob Bell calls this "turning the gem."[1]

When we're handed a workload or list of tasks, it's our responsibility to recognize everything has more to offer than we first see. For any moment, task, or relationship, we get to choose the perspective we adopt. Pick up the thing in front of you as if it were a gem, turn it, and watch how the light hits it from another angle. See where the light passes through. Change your perspective on the opportunity you have in front of you.

We add real value by (1) recognizing any contribution we make has the potential to matter and (2) accepting that we have complete control over our attitude and the quality of our contribution. We stumble upon a grand adventure when we commit to work we were not excited about in a way that adds value no one was expecting.

We're not always handed the kind of role or responsibilities we want in our careers. Often we're tasked with doing "regular work." This is great news because most of life is kind of regular. Yet we can learn to turn the gem and create something extraordinary. This ability to turn ordinary into extraordinary comes simply from a willingness to see the opportunity in each moment to create meaning for ourselves and others.

Complicated? No. Still magical? Absolutely.

Each time I've practiced this, I've grown because I decided to contribute instead of pondering why everyone isn't catering to my needs.

Even if you *really* don't want to do the work you've been assigned, you can use this approach of turning the gem. This will help you overcome feelings of frustration that may come from doing work you feel is meaningless, and it will give you a way to inject your own meaning into it. What we've already discovered in our journey bears repeating here: When we bring consciousness to our emotions and desire for substance, we can be couriers of meaning by making regular contributions in a new way. It's our gift.

Let's dive into some strategies to change the way you approach your work.

NOTE

1.   Rob Bell, *What Is the Bible?* (HarperOne, 2019).

CHAPTER 21

Finding Meaning by Making Regular Contributions

Even after years of practicing this book's principles, it's worth repeating that all of my work doesn't always feel magical. More importantly, I've learned to stop expecting to find absolute fulfillment in any personal or professional endeavor. Life just doesn't work that way. On any given week, portions of my work still seem like a series of obligations I don't feel emotionally excited to meet. When I'm unconscious to my default tendencies, I carry all of my ego's entitlement, shame, and defectiveness into my work, which causes me to not want to participate and makes the whole ordeal about me.

I have a friend who feels the same way. "Sometimes it takes me half a day to remember that, for the most part, I like work," he says. "I like making progress. I like building things. But I don't remember this until I remind myself. And most days, the only way to remind myself is to get started."

When we're down on ourselves and our abilities, we're down on our work. When we wish our tasks were more emotionally fulfilling, our emotions hijack our ability to contribute. But there are ways to overcome this. It begins with how we think about our work and ends with our willingness to view seemingly mundane tasks as invitations to contribute in a meaningful way.

I've outlined some tactics to help you get started so the rest of us can benefit from your gifts.

A MINDSET FOR REFRAMING OUR WORK

We will stop viewing work as an infringement on our freedom or a reminder we don't have what it takes when we remember our ego wants us to disengage from our lives. This reframing will allow us to be grateful for the opportunity to participate, which is the only way we'll ever prove to ourselves we're capable. Work is a gift if we believe it is. Conversely, work is a burden if we believe it is.

People like us often need to be reminded of our keen ability to shape how we see the world. We are skilled at romanticizing our lives—often to our detriment. The good news is that we can also decide to use our powerful connection to our feelings to uncover meaning from even the most ordinary jobs.

As you approach your work, ask yourself, "Where is the gift hidden in this work? What meaning is present? What purpose can I tune into? How can this unsavory set of circumstances be part of a story I get to tell one day about overcoming obstacles?"

Start with your mindset.

GETTING CLEAR ABOUT WHAT NEEDS TO BE DONE

How often do you procrastinate until you *feel* like tackling the work on your plate?

Us emotional types believe the perfect workday involves us feeling emotionally invested in everything we've got to do before we begin. But we know by now that we're not going to always feel emotionally connected with what must be done. That's why it's important to clarify what needs to happen, and in what order.

Most often the culprit of our inaction is that we feel overwhelmed and don't know where to start. If we feed the emotion of overwhelm, it becomes our reality and we spin a fantasy to avoid next steps, thus sabotaging ourselves. People like you and me often avoid actions we believe to be ordinary or obvious because we falsely believe our unique defects require magical solutions. This is not the case. We're no more or less capable than anyone else of getting clear on what needs to be done.

With that in mind, don't roll your eyes at the simplicity of the following exercise. Give it a go and make it your own. It's impossible to navigate every day perfectly, but on my best days, I follow a method we'll call the *Daily 1-2-3*.

Here's how you can put it into practice:

To begin, make a list of all of the things you need to get done. You can jot them all down in a notebook or create a note on your phone or computer. Then, on a new page or note, pull six—and only six—items from the larger list, categorizing them this way:

1. THE TOP PRIORITY

- Schedule **1** high-priority target per day.
- This takes 60 minutes to 2 hours to complete.
- It requires uninterrupted focus, your full attention.
- If you accomplished nothing else, the day would still be a success.
- Think: creative work, research, or analytical labor.
- Schedule this for a time when your energy is the highest.

2. TWO KEY OBJECTIVES REQUIRING ATTENTION TODAY

- Schedule **2** additional objectives per day that need to happen.
- They should take 45 to 60 minutes to complete.
- These tasks also require protected focus, where you're not distracted.
- This is likely incremental work on larger objectives.
- Think: drafting copy, updating a website, or preparing an agenda.

- You should have a moderate amount of gas in the tank for these items.

3. THREE NECESSARY TASKS YOU'D ALSO LIKE TO KNOCK OUT

- Schedule **3** lower-priority tasks, requiring less time, per day.
- They should require only 20 to 30 minutes to complete.
- These items help you move the week forward.
- They can be done between larger tasks.
- Think: correspondence, quick edits, or life stuff (e.g., paying bills).
- These tasks can be delegated or delayed without having a negative impact.

That's it—six items total: one top priority, two key objectives, and three necessary tasks. I've tried a dozen planners and productivity systems with more bells and whistles, but for me—a highly emotional and often unmotivated person—this is what works.

This should take you no more than five minutes to write up as you sit down to start your work. Ideally, the second you've drafted your *Daily 1-2-3*, you can begin working on your number-one priority for the day.

Here's an example of what my *Daily 1-2-3* looked like on the day I wrote this:

1. *Top Priority*
   - Finish draft of chapter for the "New Relationship with Work" section.

2. *Key Objectives*
   - Finish and send proposal to speak at credit union conference.
   - Email follow-up with five organizations I'd like to speak at in the fall.

3. *Necessary Tasks*
   - 30 minutes of email inbox catch-up.
   - Book hotel for last leg of honeymoon.
   - Write thank you notes to clients from this month.

That's a whole workday.

When you add it all up, my top priority takes two-ish hours, I'll spend about forty-five minutes tops on each of the two key objectives, and my three necessary tasks will probably take an hour total. We're talking about five hours of work to move everything forward with clarity.

I can hear the objections now . . .

- My day is full of meetings. I'll never be able to protect two hours of focused time on any one task!
- It must be nice to work for yourself. I work for an employer who micromanages my time.

- All of the things I need to accomplish fall into the number-one top priority category.

Please know that I hear you and empathize with all of those challenges (and others not mentioned). But may I still encourage you to push forward? If you're really sick of feeling like you can't get your day started because you don't know what you're supposed to do first, give the *Daily 1-2-3* a try and modify it to meet your needs.

There is no ideal process, there are no perfect circumstances, and every plan requires flexibility and fine-tuning. I ask you to remember the important practice of participating in your life. Show up, take five minutes to make a list that suits you, and begin. Whatever you end up doing is going to be a marked improvement over going down your internal elevator and wasting precious hours or days because you don't have a plan for getting started.

USING FAKE IT FOR FIVE TO FIND THE MOTIVATION TO GET STARTED

Starting is always the hardest part. But as we've learned, motivation comes to those who take action, regardless of whether they feel like it. If you've made your *Daily 1-2-3* but can't seem to start the items on your list, I'd suggest employing the *Fake It for Five* strategy we previously covered. That will help you shift your mindset and dive into the day ahead. Here's a quick review:

- Identify an activity you need to begin.
- Start a timer for five minutes.
- Play the part of a person who is motivated to do the thing you've got to do.
- Focus on the task at hand without distraction for five minutes.
- Take a quick break when time is up. (Or keep going if you're motivated!)
- Repeat.

If you actually do this, you'll find you don't want to take a break after five minutes. You'll realize you don't want to waste any more time. You'll see how action has saved you from your emotions and self-doubt.

Sometimes I'll throw in a quick sixty-second meditation before I start the five-minute timer. I'll visualize myself getting started with excitement and pushing through distractions. If this works for you, great.

Here's the bottom line: I've found motivation shows up in the midst of doing the thing we need to do, not before. Trust me. You'll be more motivated to continue with the practice once you've experienced the same.

Still not motivated, and think you need to be? Consider the alternative to taking action before you feel ready. As Shane Parrish, who authors the *Brain Food* newsletter, puts it: "Some people spend their entire lives waiting for the right moment to get started."

FINDING FOCUS WITH THE POMODORO TECHNIQUE

Just because we have a *Daily 1-2-3* doesn't guarantee we'll stick to it.

We can spend our days wading through distractions. So to keep up momentum, we must become aware of what throws us off course.

What is it for you?

- Email, interoffice chats, text messages?
- News, blogs, YouTube channels devoted to home renovation?
- Social media?
- Tidying the house, clipping your toenails, going through that pile of mail on the counter?
- Wallowing in emotions, fantasies, and false beliefs that everyone is judging you?

I'm guilty of all the above.

We give in to distractions because we believe there is going to be an emotional payoff greater than the reward we'll receive from doing what must be done. But remember, our behaviors shape our beliefs. The more we behave in a way that allows us to stay engaged and don't give in to distractions for cheap hits of dopamine, the more we'll believe we are the kind of person who can get things done and find joy in forward motion.

Once you perfect the *Fake It for Five* strategy, it's time to start harnessing the power of the "Pomodoro Technique."[1] Developed by Italian consultant and time-management expert Francesco Cirillo in the late 1980s, the Pomodoro Technique involves setting a kitchen timer for twenty-five minutes and focusing on only one thing during that time. Cirillo's kitchen timer was shaped like a tomato, or *pomodoro* in Italian.

When the twenty-five minutes are up, take a break.

As with most of the strategies in this book, it's painfully simple, which might cause us to discount its power. But nearly everything good for us is simple. The difficult part is the execution.

The most focused people we envy do not possess extra willpower, the gift of more confidence, or the ability to stay focused for longer periods of time. They simply choose to protect time to do the most important thing, then move on to the next.

Pomodoros help us take action in reasonable increments. Sometimes I avoid starting a twenty-five-minute pomodoro for forty-five minutes. But I promise you, once I begin and focus on nothing else for a full twenty-five minutes, it's always worth it.

Gloria Mark, a professor at the University of California, Irvine, and an expert on attention, conducted a study on distractions in partnership with Microsoft. Her research revealed that when we are on a computer connected to the internet, we're distracted every forty seconds. We can't even go a minute without being pulled in a different direction.

Imagine what you could do if you strung together a few pomodoros? After each twenty-five-minute session, take a quick stretch break, check your email, scroll Instagram real quick, then do another one.

KILLING THE FANTASY OF PERFECT CIRCUMSTANCES

I've always been an early morning guy.

I am more focused in the predawn hours and do my best work before sunrise. Problem is, any morning I'm not up early, I tell myself I'm not going to accomplish very much. *This day is already shot,* I'll think.

For a season of life, I blamed poor performance on my mornings going awry. Every day felt like a race to get to work. If I wasn't able to get to my tasks quickly enough, what was the use of even trying? *Might as well regroup and do things right tomorrow,* I'd tell myself.

Creating systems and routines for ourselves is a great way to increase productivity. But what happens when the best-laid plans fall through? Can we still be counted on to deliver? We must learn to believe we are capable of great contributions even when our circumstances don't seem to align.

Us emotional types tend to be all-in or all-out kinds of people:

- Either I have my morning routine or I'm not going to have a productive day.

- Either I make it to that workout class or I'm not moving my body today.
- Either I get the chance to talk through my ideas with a trusted colleague before an important meeting or I'm not going to share my ideas at all.

As we evolve in our ability to show up for work, we're going to create strategies that help us take action more effectively. That's major progress. To grow from there, we must be prepared for the moments our previous sources of motivation or security are unavailable to us—and contribute anyway.

COLLABORATING + CONNECTING TO FIND ACCOUNTABILITY

We already know we can sometimes be loners. We can drift into our internal world to avoid participating at work just as we might with other obligations. We isolate and try to do all our work alone. We obsess over perfection because we want to avoid negative feedback. Whether we worry about what others might think of our contributions or we don't want to be held accountable for a new idea, we've got to stop going it alone if we want to find fulfillment in work.

I've found collaboration and connection brings life and brightness to our professional lives. We can only do so much alone. There comes a point when we must verbalize where we're trying to go and enlist the support and accountability of others to keep us on track and motivated.

In her book *The Four Tendencies*, Gretchen Rubin—who writes and speaks about habits, happiness, and human nature—shares four categories we fall into when it comes to accountability and effectiveness.[2] I've found this helpful in my own professional journey.

The four types, in brief, are as follows:

The Upholder: Easily holds themselves accountable and follows through on promises to others. These folks always meet deadlines for work and are consistent with personal goals like exercise.

The Obliger: Favors external sources of accountability and has more difficulty with keeping themselves motivated. They love the accountability a team demands but are wishy-washy with their own desires, like creative projects or health goals, that aren't tied to public deadlines.

The Questioner: Often seems to rebel against tasks given to them. But they're really trying to rationalize their importance. If their organization's objectives make sense, they're all-stars. If they truly believe meditation will help their life, they don't miss a day. But if they can't understand the importance of something, don't expect much out of them.

The Rebel: Actively resists accountability on all fronts. They prefer following their own intuition and don't enjoy being told what to do at work. They're also not interested in setting internal goals they might not want to be committed to long term.

As someone who is driven by emotions, shame, and a desire to feel like I'm on the right track, I'm definitely an Obliger.

I've found it's exciting to share what I'm doing with others, but I need a bit of a nudge to move things across the finish line. When I'm unhealthy, I can reject any form of accountability because I see it as an opportunity for others to make me feel shame. But when we're conscious, we remember no one is out to get us, and our goal is to participate.

This very book is an example of the power of external accountability. In order to get this thing published, I emailed members of my newsletter and asked them to be readers. I promised them chapters each week that they expected me to produce and send their way. Some weeks I was a little late getting chapters out, but they still got written. The work got done. And in the midst of it all, I received encouragement and helpful critique, and I formed a bond with those who were interested in journeying together.

When we stop protecting ourselves from accountability because we worry we won't be able to meet the demands of others (for fear of shame), we see how beautiful it is to engage in work—not only for our own sake, but for the sake of all of us.

SHIPPING BEFORE YOU'RE READY

Author, speaker, and marketing expert Seth Godin is famous for plenty of concepts, but perhaps his most impactful idea involves what he describes as *shipping*. A company ships a product out the door, and in the same way, Godin pushes us to ship our ideas into the world—even when we don't think they are perfect.[3]

This is particularly helpful for you and me because we look for every excuse to delay completing and sharing our project a little longer. We wait . . . and wait until we feel emotionally ready to release our creations into the world. Often we avoid sharing our work altogether because we're afraid of the critique we might get.

When we're unconscious, we worry about putting any-thing out there because we fear someone might say it's not good. That can make us feel ashamed, reinforce our belief we are defective, and throw us back on the roller coaster of negative emotions. But when we've done the work to bring awareness and acceptance to our tendencies, we can summon the power of participation and take inspiration from the importance of sharing what we make for the ben-efit of others.

Even if it's not perfect yet.

Even if it's not unique enough yet.

Even if it feels inauthentic.

We ship it out the door before it's ready.

Otherwise, what do we have? A decade of desires still trapped inside of us, reinforcing our sense of inadequacy.

Even if someone has something negative to say about your contribution, their feedback represents their point of view. That's it. If some nasty person does wish to bring you down, you now have the tools to remind yourself you are whole as you are. You're not defined by others.

So take the presentation you've been sitting on and ship it out for feedback—even if it's only 80 percent done; publish the social media post about the idea you're interested in and get others' takes while you're thinking it through; or propose a solution to a problem you see in your organization before you've fully worked out all the steps.

Your learning, confidence, and connection to others only come from shipping something real into the world so others can interact with it.

SEEING FEEDBACK FOR THE GIFT THAT IT IS

We could spend chapters covering how to help people like us get better at receiving feedback. Heck, that could be its own book. So let's keep it simple for now.

Because we fear we're defective, we can struggle mightily with feedback. This is dangerous territory for us and for those delivering that feedback. Think about how easily we get our feelings hurt when someone doesn't treat us how we want to be treated in our personal life. This same tendency complicates our professional lives as well.

When we're overly sensitive to feedback, our employment status and reputation can certainly be affected, but, more deeply, our retreat from honest conversation about our performance leads to separation from others. And connection is both what we want and need to heal.

The mental framework I've been using and teaching for the past several years is rooted in the quote by author and Holocaust survivor Elie Wiesel: "The opposite of love is not hate, it's indifference."[4]

Though our egos sometimes trick us into thinking we want to be left alone, we really yearn for validation and affirmation from others. When presented with feedback, I'm now viewing it as someone's decision to give me attention because they're interested in who I am becoming.

Regardless of whether the feedback feels good or not, I view their energy spent on me as a sign that I'm worthy of support and investment. In return, I seek to reinvest what I learn into my work, my relationships, and the way I live.

TRUSTING OTHERS WILL APPRECIATE YOUR UNIQUE CONTRIBUTION

Sometimes when I share the story about writing that newsletter for my old consulting firm, people respond with, "But I don't have that freedom in my work."

Maybe you're a data analyst or a delivery driver, or you have a controlling boss who isn't interested in unique contributions. Name your reason. It's easy for us to make excuses about why we can't contribute in a unique way, especially if we're focused on all the ways the universe is conspiring against our special offerings.

If this is truly the case (and most times it's not), then we must focus on what we can control. We can make a regular contribution to the best of our ability while trusting that our distinct voice will color whatever it is we do. Without even trying, your imprint is on your work. Your intuition, reflectiveness, attention to detail, creative perspective, or the way you value beauty is woven into your contributions, whether you're conscious of it or not.

The kicker is that your fingerprint only becomes evident over time after you show up, do regular work, and ship normal ideas to meet ordinary deadlines. The more you focus on finding little moments of magic in mundane work, the closer you are to unlocking how to make the unique contributions only you could make.

Sometimes our work will seem to have no meaning. You may endure seasons where you don't feel fulfilled. And yet—and I hope this is clear by now—we can create meaning and find fulfillment anywhere. It is our unique gift.

There is poetry in struggle and magic in the mundane.

We must simply stick with it and endure to find what is hidden in plain sight. I hope the tactics I've shared will keep you in the game. Our greatest challenge is not finding our purpose but staying with a challenge until the purpose can be uncovered. Action—participation in work, relationships, and all other aspects of our lives—will precipitate the thoughts and feelings and ultimately help us find the meaning and connection we've always sought.

So let's not wait another moment to get started.

NOTES

1. See "Pomodoro Technique," *Wikipedia*, https://en.wikipedia.org
    /wiki/Pomodoro_Technique.
2. Gretchen Rubin, *The Four Tendencies* (Harmony, 2017).
3. Seth Godin, *The Practice: Shipping Creative Work* (Penguin
    Business, 2020).
4. Elie Wiesel in *US News & World Report* (October 27, 1986).

Accepting the Gift of Being You

I'm in Dana Point, California, for a work retreat, and the sunset dazzles then dims like a fading watercolor painting as the sand cools. Nearby, Rupert Holmes's "Escape (The Piña Colada Song)" drifts from an open-air wedding reception out to sea. I sigh with the palm trees. It still hurts to walk, and my ankle is throbbing.

I remove my orthopedic boot and hobble into the surf. Months earlier I broke my ankle, and I am just now able to start walking without the boot or the assistance of a cane. I stay for a moment in the ocean, then slowly make my way back to the fire on the beach where my coworkers are gathered. I'm peeved that no one makes a bigger deal out of my walking. I'm frustrated people pay so little attention to the way I'm navigating my life in general. I down a beer in an attempt to drink away my feelings when my coworker, Allison, comes over and asks me to dance.

Here we are again, just where we began our journey: with an invitation to dance.

Allison is one of those coworkers who quickly becomes family. We've been on the road a lot together, and she's guided me toward more confidence and, from the start, chose to connect with me in a deep way that kept me sane in a job where I felt very insecure.

She stands over me, looking at my sorry state, and informs me she'd like to crash the nearby wedding reception together. She flashes an eternal smile—like she only sees the good parts of me. She reaches her hands out, joyful, free, and fearless, and I wonder what it might be like to feel those things. I keep my hands cuffed to my drink and tell her I can't dance with this bum leg. But she's not having it.

"Dancing is exactly what you need to do. Come dance with me," she tells me. "People don't say no to me, Reagan Pugh."

She waits for me to grab her hands, and all the light from the entire evening—the fire, the moon, the wedding reception, the cars entering and exiting the parking lot—seems to emanate from her. She invites me to leave my emotions and fears behind and boogie into the story of my life.

But I refuse again and again. She grabs my forearm and I break loose. She looks at me with confused disappointment. She wants nothing more than for me to be satisfied with who I am and push through this imperfect season I'm in—but seeing her efforts will go nowhere, she leaves me where I sit. I do not dance with Allison. I do not dance for a long time, not even after my ankle is healed and I can walk normally again.

Of course, it was never my bum leg that held me back. We don't like to be presented with realities different from the ones we've constructed. My identity was so tied up in my own stories of defectiveness and the years I spent feeling like an outsider that I couldn't see things any other way.

Allison's invitation proved the most complicated of my life: Stand up and dance—there is nothing wrong with you.

I wonder, what messengers have you confused for enemies because your emotions instructed you to play the victim? Who has been rooting for you all along that you have pushed away? I hope you can now see how the belief that you're the main character in a tragic drama has been shaped by your emotions and, underneath them, by the belief that you're defective. It's easy for people like us to get lost in an internal world where we believe isolation, reflection, and brooding about all our feelings will eventually grant us freedom. We retreat, journal, listen to music, and close ourselves off from the world.

For all our self-reflection, however, we can't seem to find our way through to the truth. Flooded by emotions, we hold tighter to the belief we are broken. Instead of waking up to opportunities in front of us, we double down on old survival instincts and try to escape through the fantasy of better days in which a new relationship, job, or life situation will finally allow us to feel peace.

In reality, this fantasy pushes us further away from what we must do, which is to engage with our life as it is. We want our lives to be extraordinary. The weight of our emotions has caused us to believe we need more than ordinary living to break us free. So we avoid showing up to our normal lives and committing to the often uninspiring work of progress.

Sometimes inspiration strikes, and we feel like we finally have something to offer when we experience that rush of inspiration. But when we don't immediately follow through, shame shows up. Seeking affirmation but being unable to take the mundane steps required to turn our vision into reality, we sabotage ourselves and abandon the pursuit. That is the pattern you may be used to living out. But this is no longer our story.

This is no longer your story.

With all the awareness we've brought to your ego's default programming, I hope you can now see a different way of navigating your relationship with yourself, others, and your work. To become free, we must first get out of our internal world and show up in our lives and the lives of others. We will find the connection, belonging, and inspiration we've longed for when we stop making the story about us and our perceived flaws, when we give up the idea that others are not to be trusted.

We must stop believing our work must be unique or special for it to matter, get over our fear of being boring or ordinary, and realize we have the ability to bring meaning to any endeavor. Engaging in work and producing things in real life will reveal a path for us to naturally add value in ways we never could have expected.

We're waking up and realizing our illness has been of our own design. Our fears have been constructed to protect us from the realization that we've always been OK— and whole.

Our ego is fighting for its life by confusing us with emotions that don't represent reality, but we can see it at work now. We can see the scared parts of us trying to not be hurt again. Now with kindness, we can say, "Thank you for trying to protect me, but I don't believe there is anything wrong with me anymore. I'm stepping out."

We're also recognizing that even though our emotions aren't reality, they still have a place. With greater self-awareness, we're able to draw from our feelings to share our gifts with others.

We're not going to get this right every day, but we see that we're not the only ones who face challenges. We no longer sulk and think others have it easier than us. We realize we are no better or worse than anyone else. We accept our normalcy as a badge of honor. We smile and walk into the dance of life believing we belong on the dance floor.

Here's what I've learned over the years: Our emotional lives are complex. Wallowing in those internal experiences can keep us on the sidelines. But by being in touch with how we're feeling and showing up for others, we can help those we care about better understand themselves.

"Because of your emotions, I've learned how to have my own," my friend Veronica once told me. She was giving me a pep talk as I lamented about my lack of confidence in my writing. She and other friends saw a strength I'd overlooked.

"In your writing and the way you listen and the way you see the world, the rest of us have learned new things about ourselves," she said.

Even in the midst of my doubt and shame, my ability to articulate my emotions found a way into the life of another. My decision to participate offered light to someone else. This is what we are after. Our emotions have a place in our lives. We're just not allowing them to own us anymore.

LEARNING TO DANCE

Years after rejecting Allison's invitation to dance on the beach, I'm by the Pacific Ocean again in San Diego at a week-long conference. The entire event is about the power of meditation. Each day, through hours of meditation, we work to bring awareness to the fact that our emotions are not reality; they are simply a record of our past, as our teacher Joe Dispenza explains.

Dispenza tells us how our addiction to our emotions keeps us in a past life.[1] When we wake up each day and choose to engage with old emotions, we're reliving past wounds, traumas, and fantasies that prevent us from waking up to the freedom of the present moment. It's powerful stuff.

But if you're anything like me, regardless of the work you're doing on yourself, you enter any sort of gathering (particularly one where people are unreasonably happy) with caution. You don't want to seem too eager. You want to seem intelligent. You want to do the right things. These urges don't go away. We simply learn to become aware of them, ask if our present instincts are helpful, and choose with authority what we're going to feel, believe, and do. After a few days at the conference, my fear of what others think, my sense of defectiveness, and my desire to retreat into my internal world start to dissipate.

Every day after a break and before the next session begins, a growing dance party forms by the stage. By midweek, hundreds of people are in a mosh pit dancing to ABBA, and I begin to notice a strange urge to join them. But I ignore it for several days.

I've made a few buddies. We save seats for one another before each session. Today we're chatting in the back row waiting for the afternoon lecture to commence as the dance party rages from the front of the room. All of a sudden, a song comes on with a beat that shakes my heart.

My conference friend Linda is telling me a story, but I just can't seem to pay attention. I keep looking at the dance mob by the stage like it's a place I know filled with people I remember from another life I've yet to live. Linda stops telling her story.

"Reagan—do you need to go up there?" she asks.

The lights dim, indicating this will be the last song before the afternoon session begins, and it feels like it's the last song I might ever have the chance to dance to in my short life. I look at Linda and smile.

"I do," I say. "I do think I need to go up there."

She smiles back and pushes me so hard I almost fall backward. "Then go!"

I make my way out of our row and walk with increasing speed down the aisle toward the front of the room. With every step, my feet get hotter as I push my old story further behind me. As I approach the dance party, I swear I see a kid standing on a chair with his hands in the air and Donald Duck glasses weighing heavy on his face. His smile becomes my smile.

I push through the bodies as the strobe lights flash, the rhythm builds, and the music thumps. I'm standing still in the middle of it all as the sound intensifies and the lights go crazy. The music crescendos, then stops, and everything goes dark. The crowd begins to cheer as if we've just won a battle, like we've just recovered ground we lost long ago. I close my eyes and breathe in like I'm coming up for air after a lifetime of holding my breath.

There in the darkness I feel grateful.

I feel peace.

I feel confidence.

I feel love.

I feel new emotions—ones that have always been available to me.

I realize for the first time that I can choose helpful emotions now.

There was never anything wrong with me; I was just listening to the wrong stories.

I can see the difference now, so clearly.

The beat drops, the bass thumps even harder than before, the lights pulse back to life. I open my eyes and look around like I just woke up in the land of belonging. I'm surrounded by all these people dancing with joy—I think I see your face among them.

I keep my feet planted in place for a moment longer, turning back to—I don't know—just to see if there's something I've forgotten, something I need to bring with me.

But those old stories have brought me as far as they could.

A new story beckons.

I breathe deeply. I put my hands in the air as if I'm reaching into the light of a new future.

And I dance.

NOTE

1. Joe Dispenza, *Break the Habit of Being Yourself* (Hay House, 2013).

ACKNOWLEDGMENTS

I first want to acknowledge you, the reader. This book was written for those of us who get lost in unhelpful emotions that are rooted in a deep sense of defectiveness. Well done, you. I admire the bravery you summon each day to participate in your life and your willingness to abandon your default settings by doing the most courageous thing a human can do: believe you are whole.

To Sarah Saxton-Frump, my sister from another mister— for all the front-porch meetings and your guidance early in this book's creation, I am so very grateful. And to the people like Sarah (and me, and you, the reader) who have helped me understand my own journey by being so selfless in sharing theirs: Richard Carpenter, Karl Hébert, Aubrey Georges, and Brandon DeMaris.

To friends and collaborators who spent dedicated time helping me think about this book across its various stages— without your help clarifying the message and navigating the process, I would have given up long ago: Spud Marshall, Chris McAlister, Hudson Baird, Trevor Boehm, and David Sherry.

To the mighty group of people who subscribe to my blog and have followed my writing from the beginning—thank you for helping me build an identity as a writer with a message worth sharing.

To the writers and members of Seth Godin's Writing in Community program—I would have never captured my story or believed it could be helpful to others were it not for the accountability and encouragement I received as a member of our cohort.

To my editor Michael Schroeder—I never knew how important having an editor could be until you showed me. Then, of course, you became a trusted friend. More than helping me organize these ideas, you walked the journey with me, learned my sadness, and encouraged me to tell the story of people like me. This book would not have been completed, nor be complete, without you.

Azul Terronez, Kim Karpowitz, and the team at Authors Who Lead: Thank you for guiding me to complete this book and orchestrating the final push to bring it into the world. Connecting with y'all was no mere coincidence.

What a gift to work with clients and friends who invite me to their events and, in turn, trust me to invite their people to participate in the journey of personal growth. Specifically: Ashley Phillips, Trent McKnight, Blaze and Caroline Currie, Celya Glowacki, Christine White, Marie Spencer, Jo D. Miller, Amber Bailey, and Mamie Hertel.

To my Austin, Texas, community—y'all have influenced the content of these pages, buoyed my spirits, and offered support whether you know it or not. Specifically: Brandt Sherman, Brandon Anderson, Hudson Baird, Richard Carpenter, Ben Johanson, Sara Barge, Deleir and

Aubrey Georges, Brock Sherman, Ashlyn and Mark Hand, Tyler Burns, Chris and Amanda Covo, Mel and Brandon DeMaris, Sarah Saxton-Frump, and Clayton Stringer.

I'm eternally grateful to the mentors along the way who have invited me to grow, guided me toward participation, encouraged selflessness, and reinforced my belief in myself: John Eastham, Brittany Reese, Scott Werntz, Maleda Kunkle, Lisa Tabor, Bill Ballard, Wheelice Wilson Jr., Laura Springer, David Huffman, Earl Moseley, Lanita Legan, Terence Parker, Bill Poston, Jenna Dudevoir, Amy Kenly, Colin Speakman, Mark Updegrove, Steven Tomlinson, and Richard Ribb. Thanks for helping me grow up.

To the Austin recovery community, my little Monday-night meeting of men who want to stay sober and the welcoming arms of the fellowship of Alcoholics Anonymous.

To my family: Dad, Mom, Corbin, and Gavin. You have always been home. You accepted me at each stage of my life, regardless of my acceptance of myself. For loving me through all these years and reminding me I am whole and I belong—thank you. I wouldn't have made it this far were it not our little tribe of five.

My wife, Elle—this book is dedicated to you. How could it not be? You are endlessly dedicated to me, to your own growth, and to the life we're building together. Anytime I remark that I would have never woken up without you, you politely disagree and tell me it is I who have done the work. But, my love, I would have never have believed I could participate in the work were it not for your patience, kindness, and endless grace.

Finally, to all the younger versions of me who were afraid to participate, fearful of rejection, and unsure about making a contribution—it's OK. You experienced pain, yes, but you're learning to see more clearly now, one day at a time. You're choosing to wake up and commit to the work of realizing there's nothing wrong with you. Look at what an adventure your life has become.

EXTRA SPECIAL ACKNOWLEDGMENTS

In the book, I mentioned that there was a group of readers who agreed to review chapters on a weekly basis as this manuscript was fleshed out. Their feedback can be found implemented on every page, and their encouragement is the reason you're holding this book in your hands.

The thirteen individuals listed below deserve their own section. It is through the commitment of these folks that my commitment to this project was renewed. Thank you all, from the bottom of my heart.

Please give them a round of applause.

Andrew Henley

Andrew Seibel

Ashlyn Hand

Austin Locke

Bill Duffy

Blaze Currie

Caitlin Solano

Dionicio (Don) Flores

Lanita Legan

Nathan Ehrmann

Nathanael Pugh

Sam Whiteside

Yryskeldi Emilbek uulu

ABOUT THE AUTHOR

Photo by Richard Carpenter

Reagan Pugh is a writer, keynote speaker, and workshop facilitator with a desire to help you better understand yourself so you can have healthier relationships, contribute at a high level, and live a more meaningful life.

Pugh delivers keynote speeches and workshops to thousands of people each year and has worked with organizations like Facebook, Pepsi, Whirlpool, Cardinal Health, all branches of the US Military, Meals on Wheels, and the American Red Cross. Prior to writing and speaking full time, Reagan guided programs on storytelling and culture at companies like Nike, Western Digital, and Kimberly Clark as Chief Storyteller for a global management consulting firm.

From 2009 to 2011, Reagan served as a tenth-grade English teacher with Teach for America on the Rosebud Reservation in South Dakota. During that time, he also launched a theater program that, in its inaugural year, won the state one-act play competition for the first time.

Reagan has instructed at Texas State University, Trinity University, and Angelo State University. He continues to prioritize speaking to student audiences throughout the United States, having visited over fifty college campuses to date.

Reagan is a TEDx speaker and frequent podcast guest, and he secretly publishes poetry under a pen name (ask him about this). He lives with his wife, Elle, and their white Labrador, Lily, in Austin, Texas.

If you resonated with this book and found it helpful,
please let others know by leaving a REVIEW on Amazon.

Reagan would also love to hear from you directly!
Feel free to send him an email at reagan@reaganpugh.com
or connect with him on social media @reaganpugh.

Read more of Reagan's writing at

REAGANPUGH.COM

where you can also find more information
about booking Reagan to speak at your
event or work with your team.